Ordnance Survey

C000194046

Cycle

23 one-day routes in

North York Moors and Teesside

Compiled by
Nick Cotton

PHILIP'S

TOURS

Contents

On-road routes

Back cover photograph: Standing stones between Osmotherley and Hawnby

First published 1997 by

Ordnance Survey and George Philip Ltd, an imprint of
Romsey Road / Reed Books
Maybush / Michelin House
Southampton / 81 Fulham Road
SO16 4GU / London SW3 6RB

Text and compilation
Copyright © Reed International Books Ltd 1997
Maps Copyright © Crown Copyright 1997

The route maps in this book are based upon Ordnance Survey® Landranger® mapping.

The cross-profile diagrams in this book have been created using Ordnance Survey® Land-Form PANORAMA™ Digital height data.

Ordnance Survey and Landranger are registered trade marks and Land-Form PANORAMA is a trade mark of Ordnance Survey, the National Mapping Agency of Great Britain.

First edition 1997

A catalogue record for this atlas is available from the British Library

ISBN 0 600 59103 4
Printed in Spain

Acknowledgements
AA Photo Library 20, 25, 43, 85 • Joe Cornish 136 • Nick Cotton 59, 73
Derek Forss 99 • David Tarn back cover, 34, 37, 51, 61, 91, 106, 115, 122, 126, 133 • Judy Todd 67 • Yorkshire Tourist Board 79
• edited by Melissa Arnison-Newgass • designed by Jo Tapper
• picture research by Jenny Faithfull • production by Claudette Morris
• art editor: James Hughes

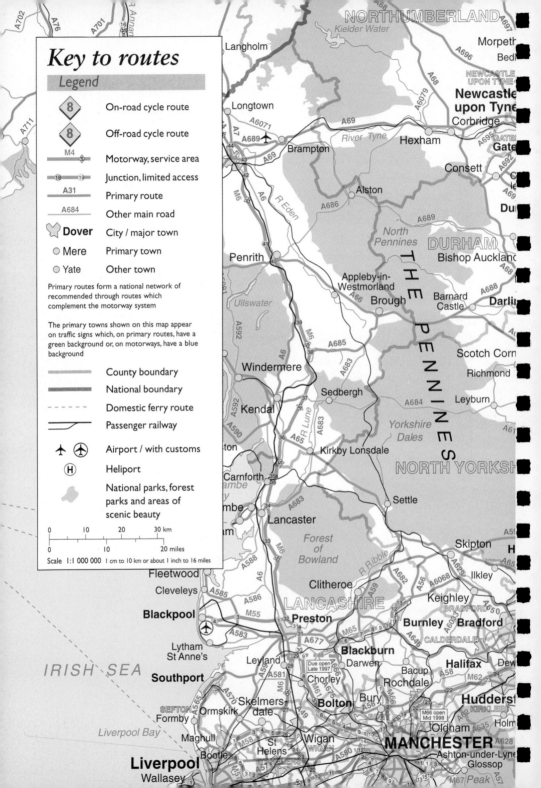

Key to routes

Legend

8	On-road cycle route
8	Off-road cycle route
M4 S	Motorway, service area
18 19	Junction, limited access
A31	Primary route
A684	Other main road
Dover	City / major town
Mere	Primary town
Yate	Other town

Primary routes form a national network of recommended through routes which complement the motorway system

The primary towns shown on this map appear on traffic signs which, on primary routes, have a green background or, on motorways, have a blue background

	County boundary
	National boundary
	Domestic ferry route
	Passenger railway
✈ ✈	Airport / with customs
H	Heliport
	National parks, forest parks and areas of scenic beauty

Scale 1:1 000 000 1 cm to 10 km or about 1 inch to 16 miles

0 10 20 30 km
0 10 20 miles

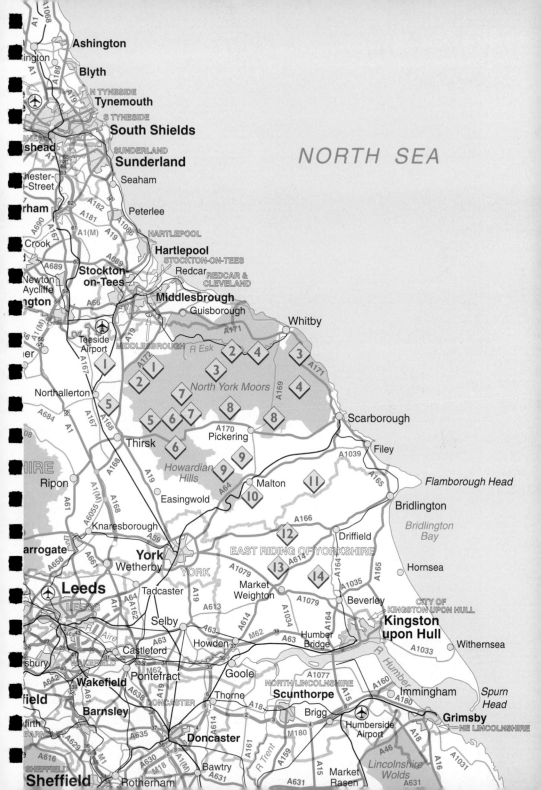

Quick reference chart

[1] **Links with other routes** Use this information to create a more strenuous ride or if you are planning to do more than one ride in a day or on a weekend or over a few days. The rides do not necessarily join: there may be a distance of about 5 km (3 miles) between the closest points. Several rides are in pairs, sharing the same starting point, which may be a good place to base yourself for a weekend.

[2] **Tourist Information Centres** You can contact them for details about accommodation. If they cannot help, there are many books that recommend places to stay. If nothing is listed for the place where you want to stay, try phoning the post office or the pub in the village to see if they can suggest somewhere. * Open from Easter to the end of September only.

North York Moors and Teesside

Although less dramatic and less mountainous than the Yorkshire Dales or the Lake District, the Yorkshire Moors and Wolds nevertheless offer a wider variety of cycling than their more illustrious cousins to the west, and, with fewer visitors, are less likely to suffer from traffic congestion on the lanes, or overcrowding and conflict with walkers on the off-road routes. The off-road routes are concentrated to the north of the region where the bridleways and byways on the moors are more plentiful, better waymarked and better maintained with an underlying geology that tends to be more cycle-friendly than the heavier soils to the south.

The wolds are the quiet ending of the chalk lands which cross Britain from Dorset via Wessex and the Chilterns, through Cambridgeshire and Lincolnshire to reach the coast north of the Humber at the dramatic cliffs of Flamborough Head. The wolds are best explored on the maze of quiet, superbly graded lanes that allow you to climb gently to the top of the rolling hills that never rise above 250 m (820 ft). There are five on-road routes through the wolds – all of which could be linked without too much difficulty. The attractive town of Beverley would be a good base to the south and Pocklington and Market Weighton are well placed to the west. Be warned that when the wind is from the North Sea it comes unobstructed by any higher ground between the Wolds and central Russia!

The moors, also known as the Hambleton Hills in the west and the Cleveland Hills in the north, are a vast expanse of heather-clad upland rising to almost 457 m (1500 ft) in the north on Urra Moor and provide much tougher challenges. Four of the on-road routes and six of the off-road routes start from the fringes of the moors and make their way into the heart of the hills. One of the finest tracks in the whole area is Rudland Rigg. On a fine day, with good visibility and light winds, this would be a ride to convince waverers and doubters of the joys of mountain biking: a real roof of the world experience on a broad, stone-based track. Other off-road routes explore the disused railway between Whitby and Scarborough, with fabulous sea views between Robin Hood's Bay and Ravenscar; the Forestry Commission routes through Langdale Forest and the small range of hills known as the Howardian Hills with the magnificent stately pile of Castle Howard at the eastern end. Thirsk, Helmsley, Kirkbymoorside, Malton and Pickering are all solid, handsome, stone-built towns and would make good bases for exploring the area over a few days.

Abbreviations and instructions

Instructions are given as concisely as possible to make them easy to follow while you are cycling. Remember to read one or two instructions ahead so that you do not miss a turning. This is most likely to occur when you have to turn off a road on which you have been riding for a fairly long distance and these junctions are marked **Easy to miss** to warn you.

If there appears to be a contradiction between the instructions and what you actually see, always refer to the map. There are many reasons why over the course of a few years instructions will need updating as new roads are built and priorities and signposts change.

If giving instructions for road routes is at times difficult, doing so for off-road routes can often be almost impossible, particularly when the route passes through woodland. With few signposts and buildings by which to orientate yourself, more attention is paid to other features, such as gradient and surface. Most of these routes have been explored between late spring and early autumn and the countryside changes its appearance very dramatically in winter. If in doubt, consult your map and check your compass to see that you are heading in the right direction.

Where I have encountered mud I have mentioned it, but this may change, not only from summer to winter but also from dry to wet weather, at any time during the year. At times you may have to retrace your steps and find a road alternative.

Some routes have small sections that follow footpaths. The instructions will highlight these sections where you must get off and push your bike. You may only ride on bridleways and by-ways so be careful if you stray from the given routes.

Directions	
L	left
LH	left-hand
RH	right-hand
SA	straight ahead or straight across
bear L or R	make less than a 90-degree (right-angle) turn at a fork in the road or track or at a sharp bend so that your course appears to be straight ahead; this is often written as *in effect SA*
sharp L or R turn	is more acute than 90 degrees
sharp R/L back on yourself	an almost U-turn
sharp LH/RH bend	a 90-degree bend
R then L or R	the second turning is visible then immediately L from the first
R then 1st L	the second turning may be some distance from the first; the distance may also be indicated: *R, then after 1 mile L*

Junctions

T-j	T-junction, a junction where you have to give way
X-roads	crossroads, a junction where you may or may not have to give way
offset X-roads	the four roads are not in the form of a perfect cross and you will have to turn left then right, or vice versa, to continue the route

Signs

'Placename 2'	words in quotation marks are those that appear on signposts; the numbers indicate distance in miles unless stated otherwise
NS	not signposted
trig point	a trigonometrical station

Instructions

An example of an easy instruction is:

4 At the T-j at the end of Smith Road by the White Swan PH R on Brown Street 'Greentown 2, Redville 3'.

There is more information in this instruction than you would normally need, but things do change: pubs may close down and signs may be replaced, removed or vandalized.

An example of a difficult instruction is:

8 Shortly after the brow of the hill, soon after passing a telephone box on the right next L (NS).

As you can see, there is no T-junction to halt you in your tracks, no signpost indicating where the left turn will take you, so you need to have your wits about you in order not to miss the turning.

Fact boxes

The introduction to each route includes a fact box giving useful information:

Start

This is the suggested start point coinciding with instruction I on the map. There is no reason why you should not start at another point if you prefer.

Distance and grade

The distance is, of course, that from the beginning to the end of the route. If you wish to shorten the ride, however, the maps enable you to do so.

The number of drinks bottles indicates the grade:

Easy

Moderate

Strenuous

Page diagrams

The on-road routes usually occupy four pages of mapping each. The page diagrams on the introductory pages show how the map pages have been laid out, how they overlap and if any inset maps have been used.

This section of the route is shown on pages 92 and 93

This overlap area appears at the foot of pages 92 and 93 and at the top of pages 94 and 95

This area is shown as an inset on page 94

This section of the route is shown on pages 94 and 95

92   93

94   95

The grade is based on the amount of climbing involved.

Remember that conditions may vary dramatically with the weather and seasons, especially along off-road sections

Terrain

This brief description of the terrain may be read in conjunction with the cross-profile diagram at the foot of the page to help you to plan your journey.

Nearest railway

This is the distance to the nearest station from the closest point on the route, not necessarily from the start. Before starting out you should check with British Rail for local restrictions regarding the carrying of bicycles.
(See page 15)

Refreshments

Pubs and teashops on or near the route are listed. The tankard symbols indicate pubs particularly liked by the author.

Before you go

Preparing yourself

Fitness

Cycling uses muscles in a different way from walking or running, so if you are beginning or returning to it after a long absence you will need time to train your muscles and become accustomed to sitting on a saddle for a few hours. Build up your fitness and stamina gradually and make sure you are using a bicycle that is the right size for you and suits your needs.

Equipment

Attach the following items to the bike: bell, pump, light-brackets and lights, lock-holder and lock, rack and panniers or elastic straps for securing things to the rack, map holder. Unless it is the middle of summer and the weather is guaranteed to be fine, you will need to carry extra clothes, particularly a waterproof, with you, and it is well worth investing in a rack for this purpose.

Wearing a small pouch around your waist is the easiest and safest way of carrying small tools and personal equipment. The basics are: Allen keys to fit the various Allen bolts on your bike, chainlink extractor, puncture repair kit, reversible screwdriver (slot and crosshead), small adjustable spanner, spare inner tube, tyre levers (not always necessary with mountain bike tyres), coins and a phonecard for food and telephone calls, compass.

Additional tools for extended touring: bottom bracket extractor, cone spanners, freewheel extractor, headset spanners, lubricant, socket spanner for pedals, spare cables, spoke-key.

Clothing

What you wear when you are cycling should be comfortable, allowing you, and most especially your legs, to move freely. It should also be practical, so that it will keep you warm and dry if and when the weather changes.

Feet You can cycle in just about any sort of footwear, but bear in mind that the chain has oil on it, so do not use your very best shoes. Leather tennis shoes or something similar, with a smooth sole to slip into the pedal and toe clip are probably adequate until you buy specialist cycling shoes, which have stiffer soles and are sometimes designed for use with specialist pedals.

Legs Cycling shorts or padded cycling underwear worn under everyday clothing make long rides much more comfortable. Avoid tight, non-stretch trousers, which are very uncomfortable for cycling and will sap your energy, as they restrict the movement of your legs; baggy tracksuit bottoms, which can get caught in the chain and will sag around your ankles if they get wet. Almost anything else will do, though a pair of stretch leggings is probably best.

- **Upper body** What you wear should be long enough to cover your lower back when you are leaning forward and, ideally, should have zips or buttons that you can adjust to regulate your temperature. Several thin layers are better than one thick layer.

- **Head** A helmet may protect your head in a fall.

- **Wet weather** A waterproof, windproof top is essential if it looks like rain. A dustbin bag would be better than nothing but obviously a breathable waterproof material is best.

- **Cold weather** A hat that covers your ears, a scarf around your neck, a pair of warm gloves and a thermal top and bottom combined with what you would normally wear cycling should cover almost all conditions.

- **Night and poor light** Wearing light-coloured clothes or reflective strips is almost as important as having lights on your bike. Reflective bands worn around the ankles are particularly effective in making you visible to motorists.

Preparing your bicycle

- You may not be a bicycle maintenance expert, but you should make sure that your bike is roadworthy before you begin a ride.

- If you are planning to ride in soft, off-road conditions, fit fat, knobbly tyres. If you are using the bike around town or on a road route, fit narrower, smoother tyres.

- Check the tyres for punctures or damage and repair or replace if necessary or if you are in any doubt. Keep tyres inflated hard (recommended pressures are on the side wall of the tyre) for mainly on-road riding. You do not need to inflate tyres as hard for off-road use; slightly softer tyres give some cushioning and get better traction in muddy conditions.

- Ensure that the brakes work efficiently. Replace worn cables and brake blocks.

- The bike should glide along silently. Tighten and adjust any part that is loose or rubbing against a moving part. Using a good-quality bike oil lubricate the hubs, bottom bracket, pedals where they join the cranks, chain and gear-changing mechanism from both sides. If the bike still makes grating noises, replace the bearings.

- Adjust the saddle properly. The saddle height should ensure that your legs are working efficiently: too low and your knees will ache; too high and your hips will be rocking in order for your feet to reach the pedals. Some women find the average bike saddle uncomfortable because the female pelvis is a different shape from the male pelvis and needs a broader saddle for support. Some manufacturers make saddles especially for women.

Cross-profiles

The introduction to each route includes a cross-profile diagram. The blue grid indicates 1-kilometre horizontal intervals and 50-metre vertical intervals

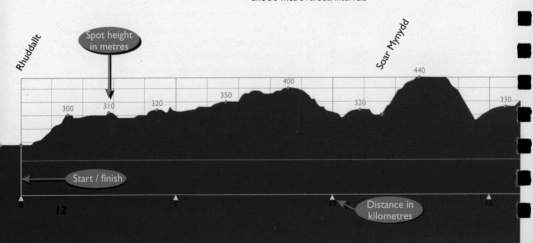

Tips for touring

The law

England and Wales have 193 000 km (120 000 miles) of rights of way, but under the Wildlife and Countryside Act of 1968 you are allowed to cycle on only about 10 percent of them, namely on bridleways, by-ways open to all traffic (BOATs) and roads used as public paths (RUPPs).

The other 90 percent of rights of way are footpaths, where you may walk and usually push your bike, but not ride it. Local bylaws sometimes prohibit the pushing of bicycles along footpaths and although all the paths in this book have been checked, bylaws do sometimes change.

⚙ You are not allowed to ride where there is no right of way. If you lose the route and find yourself in conflict with a landowner, stay calm and courteous, make a note of exactly where you are and then contact the Rights of Way Department of the local authority. It has copies of definitive maps and will take up the matter on your behalf if you are in the right.

Cycling techniques

If you are not used to cycling more than a few kilometres at a stretch, you may find initially that touring is tiring. There are ways of conserving your energy, however:

⚙ Do not struggle in a difficult gear if you have an easier one. Let the gears help you up the hills. No matter how many gears a bike has, however, ultimately it is leg power that you need to get you up a hill. You may decide to get off and walk uphill with your bike to rest your muscles.

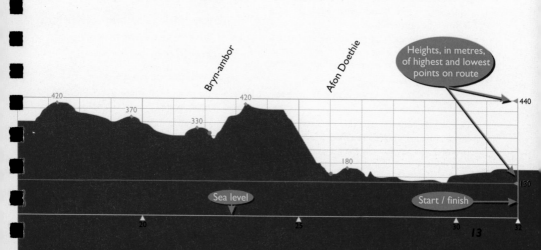

You can save a lot of energy on the road by following close behind a stronger rider in his or her slipstream, but do not try this offroad. All the routes are circular, so you can start at any point and follow the instructions until you return to it. This is useful when there is a strong wind, as you can alter the route to go into the wind at the start of the ride, when you are fresh, and have the wind behind you on the return, when you are more tired.

The main difference in technique between on-road and off-road cycling lies in getting your weight balanced correctly. When going down steep off-road sections, lower the saddle, keep the pedals level, stand up out of the saddle to let your legs absorb the bumps and keep your weight over the rear wheel. Control is paramount: keep your eyes on what lies ahead.

Traffic

The rides in this book are designed to minimize time spent on busy roads, but you will inevitably encounter some traffic. The most effective way to avoid an accident with a motor vehicle is to be highly aware of what is going on around you and to ensure that other road users are aware of you.

Ride confidently.

Indicate clearly to other road users what you intend to do, particularly when turning right. Look behind you, wait for a gap in the traffic, indicate, then turn. If you have to turn right off a busy road or on a difficult bend, pull in and wait for a gap in the traffic or go past the turning to a point where you have a clear view of the traffic in both directions, then cross and return to the turning.

Use your lights and wear reflective clothing at night and in poor light.

Do not ride two-abreast if there is a vehicle behind you. Let it pass. If it cannot easily overtake you because the road is narrow, look for a passing place or a gate entrance and pull in to let it pass.

Maintenance

Mountain bikes are generally stronger than road bikes, but any bike can suffer. To prevent damage as far as possible:

Watch out for holes and obstacles.

Clean off mud and lubricate moving parts regularly.

Replace worn parts, particularly brake blocks.

Riders also need maintenance:

Eat before you get hungry, drink before you get thirsty. Dried fruit, nuts and chocolate take up little space and provide lots of energy.

Carry a water bottle and keep it filled, especially on hot days. Tea, water and well-diluted soft drinks are the best thirst-quenchers.

Breakdowns

The most likely breakdown to occur is a puncture.

Always carry a pump.

Take a spare inner tube so that you can leave the puncture repair until later.

Make sure you know how to remove a wheel. This may require an adjustable spanner or, in many cases, no tool at all, as many bikes now have wheels with quick-release skewers that can be loosened by hand.

Security

Where you park your bike, what you lock it with and to are important in protecting it from being stolen.

Buy the best lock you can afford.

Lock your bike to something immovable in a well-lit public place.

Locking two bikes together is better than locking them individually.

Use a chain with a lock to secure the wheels and saddle to the frame. Keep a note of the frame number and other details, and insure, photograph and code the bike.

Transporting your bike

There are three ways of getting you and your bike to the start of a ride:

Cycle to the start or to a point along a route near your home.

Take the train. Always check in advance that you can take the bike on the train. Some trains allow only up to two bikes and you may need to make a reservation and pay a flat fee however long the journey. Always label your bike showing your name and destination station.

Travel by motor vehicle. You can carry the bikes:

- Inside the vehicle. With the advent of quick release mechanisms on both wheels and the seatpost, which allow a quick dismantling of the bike, it is possible to fit a bike in even quite small cars. It is unwise to stack one bike on top of another unless you have a thick blanket separating them to prevent scratching or worse damage. If you are standing them up in a van, make sure they are secured so they cannot slide around.

- On top of the vehicle. The advantages of this method are that the bikes are completely out of the way and are not resting against each other, you can get at the boot or hatch easily and the bikes do not obscure the number plate or rear lights and indicators. The disadvantages are that you use up more fuel, the car can feel uncomfortable in a crosswind and you have to be reasonably tall and strong to get the bikes on and off the roof.

- On a rack that attaches to the rear of the vehicle. The advantages are that the rack is easily and quickly assembled and disassembled, fuel consumption is better and anyone can lift the bikes on and off. The disadvantages are that you will need to invest in a separate board carrying the number plate and rear lights if they are obstructed by the bikes, you cannot easily get to the boot or hatch once the bikes have been loaded and secured, and the bikes are resting against each other so you must take care that they don't scrape off paint or damage delicate parts.

- Whichever way you carry the bikes on the outside of the vehicle, ensure that you regularly check that they are secure and that straps and fixings that hold them in place have not come loose. If you are leaving the bikes for any length of time, be sure they are secure against theft; if nothing else lock them to each other.

Code of Conduct

- Enjoy the countryside and respect its life and work
- Only ride where you know you have a legal right
- Always yield to horses and pedestrians
- Take all litter with you
- Don't get annoyed with anyone; it never solves any problems
- Guard against all risk of fire
- Fasten all gates
- Keep your dogs under close control
- Keep to public paths across farmland
- Use gates and stiles to cross fences, hedges and walls
- Avoid livestock, crops and machinery or, if not possible, keep contact to a minimum
- Help keep all water clean
- Protect wildlife, plants and trees
- Take special care on country roads
- Make no unnecessary noise

Legend to 1:50 000 maps

Roads and paths

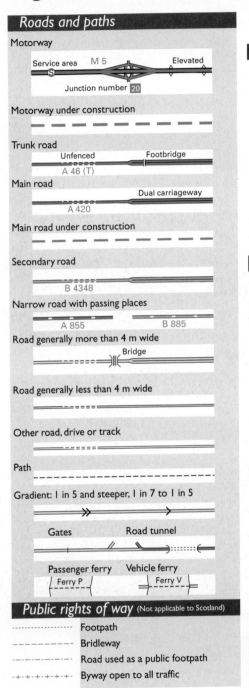

Motorway

Service area | M 5 | Elevated

Junction number 20

Motorway under construction

Trunk road

Unfenced | Footbridge

A 46 (T)

Main road

Dual carriageway

A 420

Main road under construction

Secondary road

B 4348

Narrow road with passing places

A 855 | B 885

Road generally more than 4 m wide

Bridge

Road generally less than 4 m wide

Other road, drive or track

Path

Gradient: 1 in 5 and steeper, 1 in 7 to 1 in 5

Gates | Road tunnel

Passenger ferry | Vehicle ferry

Ferry P | Ferry V

Public rights of way (Not applicable to Scotland)

.... Footpath

— — — — Bridleway

—·—·—·— Road used as a public footpath

-+-+-+-+- Byway open to all traffic

Danger Area | Firing and test ranges in the area. Danger! Observe warning notices

Tourist information

i **i** Information centre, all year / seasonal

P Parking

✗ Picnic site

☆ Viewpoint

⋏ Camp site

⚏ Caravan site

▲ Youth hostel

▨ Selected places of tourist interest

✆ Public telephone

✆ Motoring organisation telephone

⌐ Golf course or link

PC Public convenience (in rural areas)

Railways

Track: multiple or single

Track: narrow gauge

Bridges, footpath

Tunnel

Viaduct

Freight line, siding or tramway

a b

Station, (a) principal, (b) closed to passengers

LC Level crossing

Embankment

Cutting

Rock features

outcrop · cliff · 650 · 600 · scree

Public rights of way indicated by these symbols have been derived from Definitive Maps as amended by the latest enactments or instruments held by Ordnance Survey and are shown subject to the limitations imposed by the scale of mapping. Further information may be obtained from the appropriate County or London Borough Council

The representation on this map of any other road, track or path is no evidence of the existence of a right of way

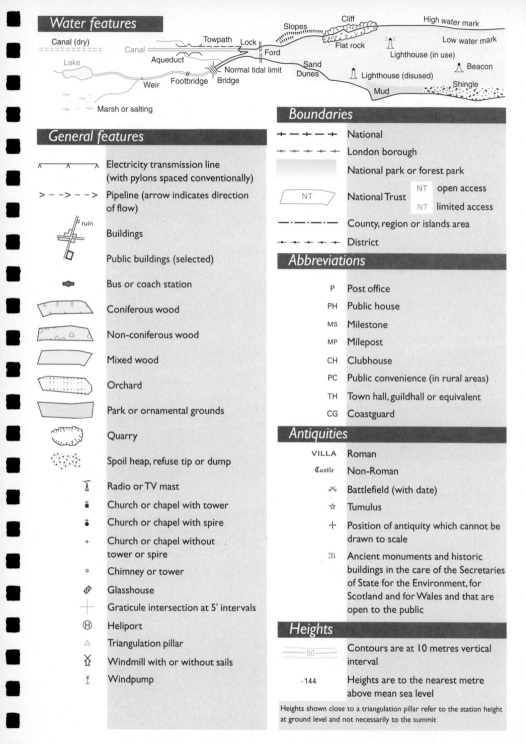

Water features

Canal (dry)

Canal

Lake

Aqueduct

Weir Footbridge Bridge

Towpath Lock

Ford

Normal tidal limit

Marsh or salting

Slopes Cliff High water mark

Flat rock Low water mark

Lighthouse (in use)

Sand Beacon
Dunes Lighthouse (disused)

Shingle

Mud

General features

∧——∧——∧ Electricity transmission line (with pylons spaced conventionally)

>-->--> Pipeline (arrow indicates direction of flow)

ruin Buildings

Public buildings (selected)

Bus or coach station

Coniferous wood

Non-coniferous wood

Mixed wood

Orchard

Park or ornamental grounds

Quarry

Spoil heap, refuse tip or dump

Ᾱ Radio or TV mast

Church or chapel with tower

Church or chapel with spire

+ Church or chapel without tower or spire

○ Chimney or tower

Glasshouse

Graticule intersection at 5' intervals

Ⓗ Heliport

△ Triangulation pillar

Windmill with or without sails

Windpump

Boundaries

+ — + — + National

-∘- -∘- -∘- -∘- London borough

National park or forest park

NT National Trust
NT open access
NT limited access

—·—·—·— County, region or islands area

+ — + — + District

Abbreviations

P Post office

PH Public house

MS Milestone

MP Milepost

CH Clubhouse

PC Public convenience (in rural areas)

TH Town hall, guildhall or equivalent

CG Coastguard

Antiquities

VILLA Roman

Castle Non-Roman

⚔ Battlefield (with date)

☆ Tumulus

+ Position of antiquity which cannot be drawn to scale

ℳ Ancient monuments and historic buildings in the care of the Secretaries of State for the Environment, for Scotland and for Wales and that are open to the public

Heights

——50—— Contours are at 10 metres vertical interval

·144 Heights are to the nearest metre above mean sea level

Heights shown close to a triangulation pillar refer to the station height at ground level and not necessarily to the summit

Between the Dales and the Moors, north of Northallerton

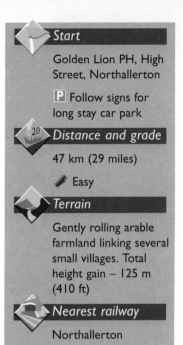

Start

Golden Lion PH, High Street, Northallerton

P Follow signs for long stay car park

Distance and grade

47 km (29 miles)

Easy

Terrain

Gently rolling arable farmland linking several small villages. Total height gain – 125 m (410 ft)

Nearest railway

Northallerton

Northallerton is the county town of North Yorkshire and boasts a fine, wide High Street with an array of old buildings. The 3 km (2 miles) at the start and finish of the ride will carry a fair amount of traffic so be prepared. Beyond Yafforth you enter a delightful maze of quiet country lanes undulating gently between 30 and 75 m (100–250 ft) with no major climbs. The route passes across rich farmland and past fine farms and red-brick barns with glimpses of the Yorkshire Moors away to the east. After passing close by the River Tees near Hornby the route turns south through the village of Appleton Wiske. The ride continues south, reaching its high point of 75 m (246 ft) near Deighton before returning to Northallerton.

NB For a longer ride which avoids Northallerton altogether, start with on-road Route 5 and follow the links described in the directions of each route.

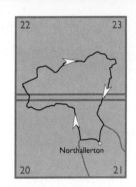

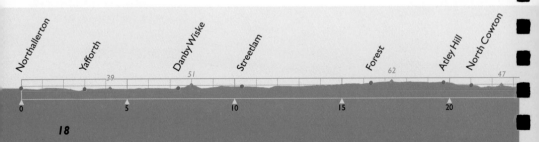

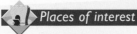

Places of interest

Northallerton 1

This old posting station retains many of its old inns (the Old Fleece Inn is partly medieval) and is famed for its beers. The town is built along a curving street, which broadens in the middle to form a market square, and narrows again at its north end near the church. There are many Georgian houses and a Victorian town hall, built in 1873, stands in the square

Kiplin Hall *just off the route near 6*

A Jacobean manor full of art treasures, where Lord Baltimore, founder of the State of Maryland, USA, once lived

Brompton 13

Attractive village surrounding a large green intersected by Brompton Beck. Sir George Cayley, landowner and squire of Brompton in the early 19th century, was an indefatigable inventor. Among his ideas were a caterpillar tractor (1825), gliders, aircraft, a hot-air engine and even a guided missile, the design of which was offered to the Duke of Wellington whose comments are unfortunately not recorded. In 1852 he sent his coachman flying across a valley in a glider fitted with many of the essential features of a modern aircraft. The poor man was too terrified to appreciate the privilege of being a pioneer of aviation and on his return to earth handed in his notice, explaining that he had been hired to drive, not fly!

Refreshments

Golden Lion PH 🍺, *plenty of choice in* **Northallerton**
Revellers Country Inn, **Yafforth**
White Swan PH 🍺, **Danby Wiske**
Beeswing PH, **East Cowton**
Bay Horse Inn, Black Bull PH, **Great Smeaton**
Grange Arms PH, **Hornby**
Lord Nelson Inn, **Appleton Wiske**
Crown PH, Three Horseshoes PH, **Brompton**

East Cowton   Great Smeaton   Hornby   Appleton Wiske   Deighton   Brompton

52   63   64   75

28

25   30   35   40   45   46.6

19

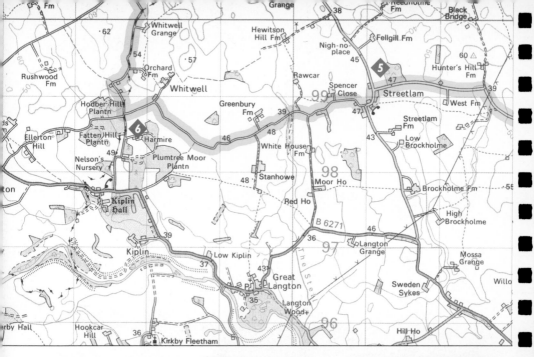

1 With back to the Golden Lion PH in Northallerton High Street R on the A167 towards Darlington and Richmond. At the roundabout SA 'Darlington A167, Richmond (B6271)'

2 At mini roundabout L on B6271 'Yafforth 1½, Scorton 10, Richmond 15'

3 Follow B6271 for 2 km (1¼ miles). Soon after the church and immediately after the Revellers Country Inn in Yafforth 1st R 'Danby Wiske 2½'

4 After 4 km (2½ miles) at X-roads in Danby Wiske L 'Streetlam 1¾, Richmond 12'

5 At T-j by red-brick bungalow L. Go past telephone box, then on sharp LH bend bear R (in effect SA) 'Whitwell 2¼, Richmond 10'

6 At offset X-roads after 4 km (2½ miles) R 'Forest 1, Atley Hill 2½'

▲ Brompton

➡ page 22

12 At T-j after 8 km (5 miles) L 'Brompton 1, Northallerton 3'

13 At X-roads in Brompton by the Crown PH R 'Northallerton 1½' (**Or** for link to on-road Route 5 continue SA at X-roads)

14 At T-j with A684 R 'Northallerton ½'

15 At 1st roundabout R 'Town Centre'. At 2nd roundabout L to return to the start

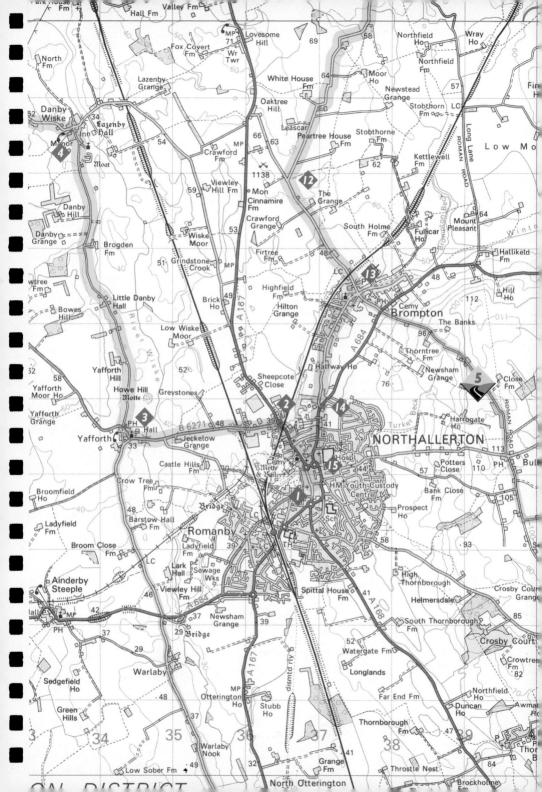

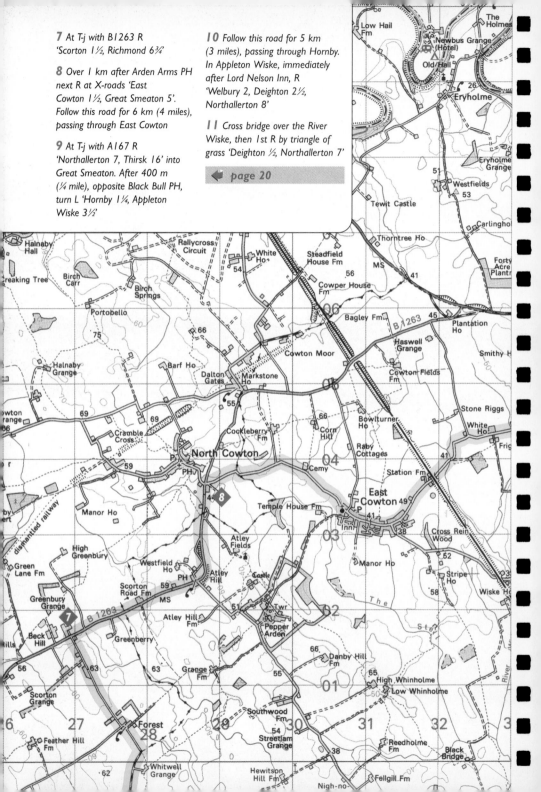

7 At T-j with B1263 R 'Scorton 1½, Richmond 6¾'

8 Over 1 km after Arden Arms PH next R at X-roads 'East Cowton 1½, Great Smeaton 5'. Follow this road for 6 km (4 miles), passing through East Cowton

9 At T-j with A167 R 'Northallerton 7, Thirsk 16' into Great Smeaton. After 400 m (¼ mile), opposite Black Bull PH, turn L 'Hornby 1¼, Appleton Wiske 3½'

10 Follow this road for 5 km (3 miles), passing through Hornby. In Appleton Wiske, immediately after Lord Nelson Inn, R 'Welbury 2, Deighton 2½, Northallerton 8'

11 Cross bridge over the River Wiske, then 1st R by triangle of grass 'Deighton ½, Northallerton 7'

◀ page 20

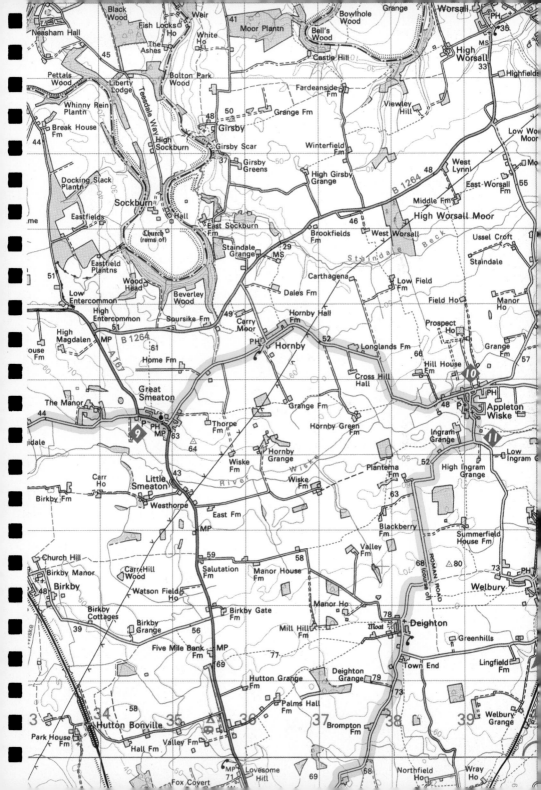

2 *High moorland, east of Osmotherley*

*F*rom Osmotherley round to Guisborough the escarpment edge of the North Yorkshire Moors is at its steepest and most spectacular, at times rising 300 m (1000 ft) in less than 2 km (1½ miles). The ride starts as it means to continue with a climb through the 'pass' in the hills known as Scarth Nick followed by a fast descent down into Swainby. After a gentle climb to Faceby and Carlton in Cleveland you are now faced with the toughest and longest ascent of the day, with one very steep section on Carlton Bank. This is high moorland country with drystone walls and heather-clad hills stretching away into the distance; an improbably situated cafe at the top of the hill near Stone Intake gives you something to aim for. The route drops down to the B1257 at Chop Gate; there are no major climbs on this section and the views are good. Once off the B1257 the ride turns into a roller-coaster of climbs and descents with one extraordinarily steep section just before Hawnby. There are two further steep dips into river valleys before you climb to the high point of the ride on the moorland above Osmotherley and enjoy the last, fast swoop down to the start.

Start

Three Tuns PH, Osmotherley, just off the A19 to the north-east of Northallerton

P No specific car park, please show consideration

Distance and grade

47 km (29 miles)

///// Strenuous

Terrain

Hills, moorland, river valleys and woodland close to Hawnby. Total height gain – 790 m (2590 ft)

Nearest railway

Northallerton, 10 km (6 miles) southwest of Osmotherley

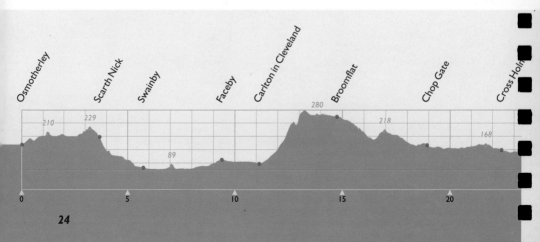

Osmotherley · Scarth Nick · Swainby · Faceby · Carlton in Cleveland · Broomflat · Chop Gate · Cross Holm

210 · 229 · 89 · 280 · 218 · 168

0 · 5 · 10 · 15 · 20

Osmotherley /

Old market centre set at the foot of the Cleveland Hills. The stone table where John Wesley preached still stands, as does the Methodist church dating from 1754 – one of England's first

Mount Grace Priory /

The best-preserved Carthusian monastery in Britain. One monk's cell has been restored. A substantial church and cloister remains

Scarth Nick 2

A nick in the hills between Osmotherley and Swainby. Scarth Wood Moor is the start of a 63-km (39-mile) section of the Cleveland Way which crosses from the moors to the coast

▲ Swainby

Refreshments

Queen Catherine Hotel, Three Tuns PH 🍴, Golden Lion PH 🍴, coffee shop, **Osmotherley**
Miners Arms PH, Blacksmiths Arms PH, Black Horse PH 🍴, **Swainby**
Cafe Martin at the Sutton Arms, **Faceby**
Blackwell Ox PH, **Carlton in Cleveland**
Lordstones Cafe at the top of the hill after **Carlton in Cleveland**
Buck PH 🍴, **Chop Gate**
Sun Inn, **Fangdale Beck**
Hawnby PH 🍴, **Hawnby**

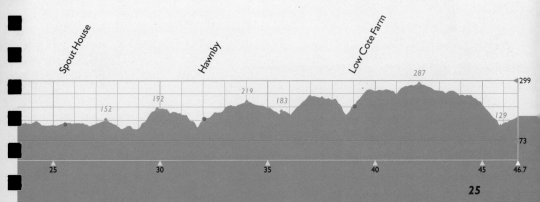

Take care not to mistake the faded yellow line of the national park boundary for the solid yellow line of the route

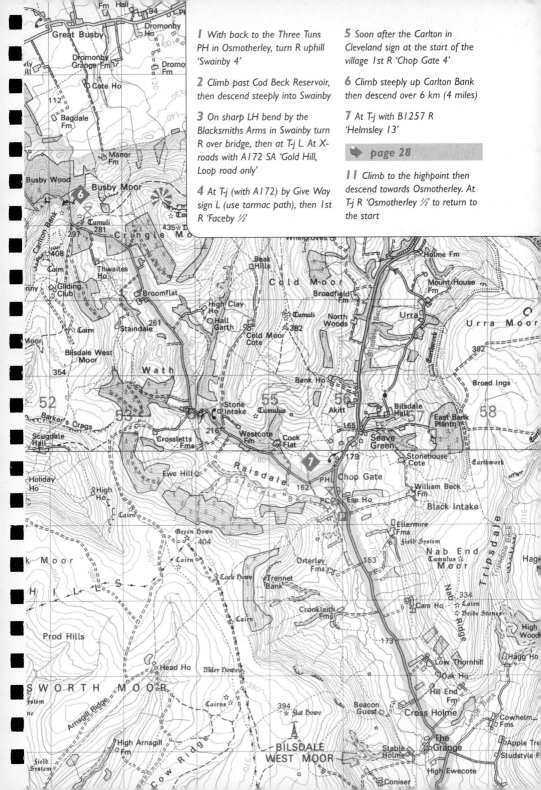

1 With back to the Three Tuns PH in Osmotherley, turn R uphill 'Swainby 4'

2 Climb past Cod Beck Reservoir, then descend steeply into Swainby

3 On sharp LH bend by the Blacksmiths Arms in Swainby turn R over bridge, then at T-j L. At X-roads with A172 SA 'Gold Hill, Loop road only'

4 At T-j (with A172) by Give Way sign L (use tarmac path), then 1st R 'Faceby ½'

5 Soon after the Carlton in Cleveland sign at the start of the village 1st R 'Chop Gate 4'

6 Climb steeply up Carlton Bank then descend over 6 km (4 miles)

7 At T-j with B1257 R 'Helmsley 13'

➡ **page 28**

11 Climb to the highpoint then descend towards Osmotherley. At T-j R 'Osmotherley ½' to return to the start

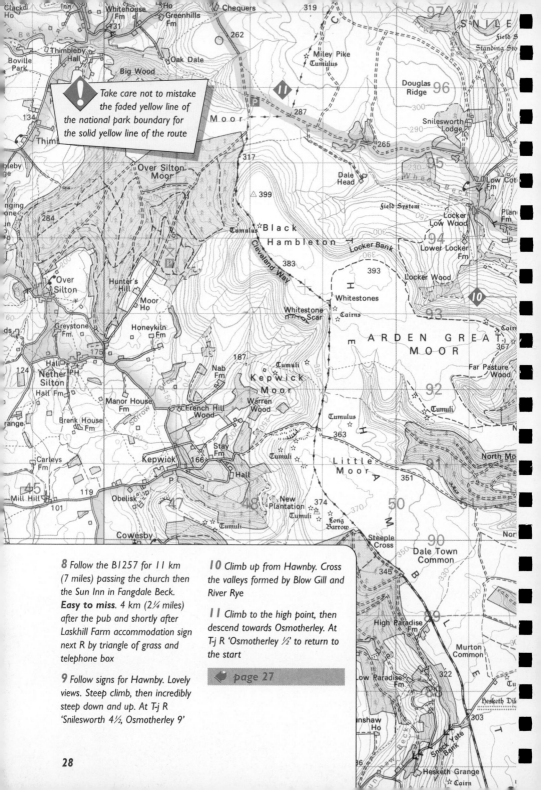

Take care not to mistake the faded yellow line of the national park boundary for the solid yellow line of the route

8 Follow the B1257 for 11 km (7 miles) passing the church then the Sun Inn in Fangdale Beck. **Easy to miss**. 4 km (2¼ miles) after the pub and shortly after Laskhill Farm accommodation sign next R by triangle of grass and telephone box

9 Follow signs for Hawnby. Lovely views. Steep climb, then incredibly steep down and up. At T-j R 'Snilesworth 4½, Osmotherley 9'

10 Climb up from Hawnby. Cross the valleys formed by Blow Gill and River Rye

11 Climb to the high point, then descend towards Osmotherley. At T-j R 'Osmotherley ½' to return to the start

page 27

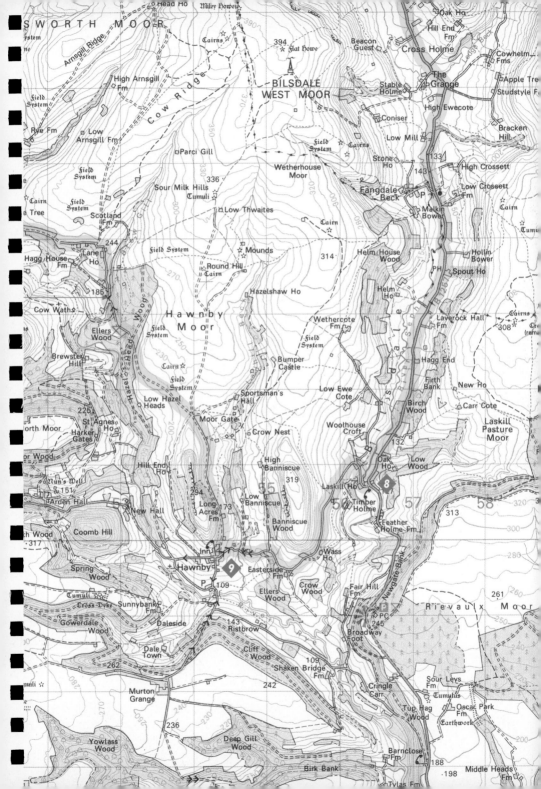

3 *A tough moorland challenge*

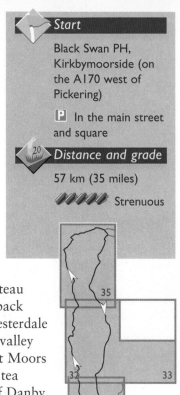

Start

Black Swan PH, Kirkbymoorside (on the A170 west of Pickering)

P In the main street and square

Distance and grade

57 km (35 miles)

Strenuous

This is the toughest on-road route in the book with almost 1210 m (4000 ft) of climbing over the highest part of the Yorkshire Moors. The ride starts from Kirkbymoorside and wastes no time in climbing north up onto the moor. You get a hint of the views to come at the end of the attractive, stone-built village of Gillamoor. Beyond the village the route descends into Farndale, strewn with daffodils in spring, then tackles the first of the very steep sections to emerge on the high moorland plateau with rolling acres of heather and fine views back down into the valleys. A fast descent into Westerdale followed by an undulating section along the valley of the River Esk take you to the well laid-out Moors Centre at Danby with its excellent adjoining tea room. A long, steady climb along the edge of Danby Dale brings you back up to the plateau and a choice of the easy route back or the full version involving one more climb out of Rosedale Abbey. Whichever you choose, the refreshment possibilities back in Kirkbymoorside will never have looked so good!

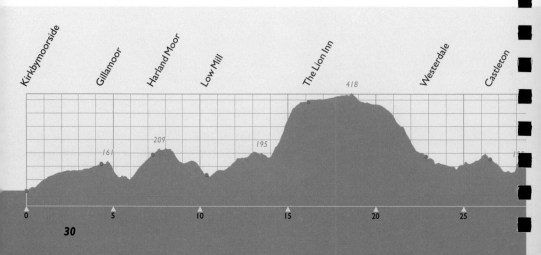

Terrain

Into the heart of the Yorkshire Moors and its heather-clad plateau, over the highest roads in the National Park, with two of the steepest climbs in the book. Total height gain – 1210 m (3970 ft)

Nearest railway

Norton, 21 km (13 miles) southeast of Kirkbymoorside

Places of interest

Kirkbymoorside 1
The village has staged a market every Wednesday for the past 6 centuries. The coaching inns include the half-timbered Black Swan of 1634

Farndale 4–6
The valley is carpeted with daffodils in spring; the local inhabitants claim that this inspired Wordsworth

Danby Rigg 12–13
Defensive dikes and some 800 cairns constructed around 1000 BC lie in the hills above Danby

Refreshments

George & Dragon PH 🍴🍴, plenty of choice in **Kirkbymoorside**
Royal Oak PH 🍴, Platters Tea Room, **Gillamoor**
Lion Inn 🍴🍴, **Blakey Ridge**
Downe Arms PH 🍴, Moorland Inn, Castleton Tea Rooms, **Castleton**
Duke of Wellington PH, tea room, **Danby**
Tea rooms at **Danby Moors Centre** (daily in summer, weekends only in winter)
Milburn Arms PH 🍴🍴, tea rooms, **Rosedale Abbey**
Crown PH 🍴, tea rooms, **Hutton-le-Hole**

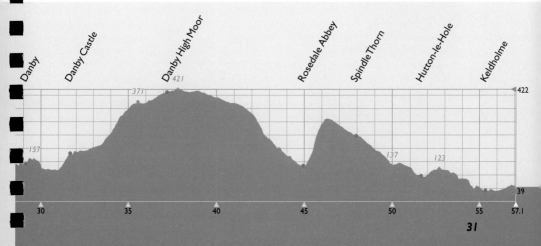

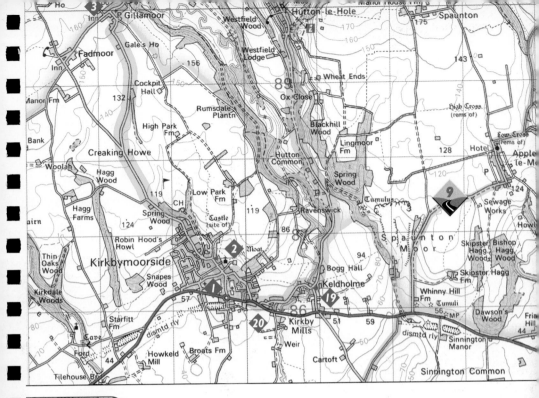

1 With back to the Black Swan PH in Kirkbymoorside L uphill 'Gillamoor 2½, Farndale'

2 At roundabout at the top of High Market Place L 'Gillamoor, Fadmoor, Farndale'

3 **Ignore** left and right turns, following signs for Gillamoor. At T-j in Gillamoor R 'Hutton-le-Hole 2½, Farndale'

4 Fine views at the end of the village. Steeply downhill. **Easy to miss**. 1st L on descent 'Farndale'

5 Follow for 5 km (3 miles). In Low Mill, near the bottom of the hill, 1st R 'Hutton-le-Hole 4, Farndale (East Side), then at T-j after bridge L

6 After 2 km (1½ miles) 1st R by triangle of grass 'Castleton 7¾ via Blakey Bank', then at T-j after 800 m (½ mile) R 'Castleton 7¼

7 At T-j at the top of very steep climb L 'Castleton 6½'

➤ **page 34**

17 Superb descent down into Rosedale Abbey. Through the village following signs for Pickering, then at the end of the village turn R 'Rosedale Chimney Bank'. Very steep climb (1:3)

18 After 6 km (4 miles), at T-j by old stone barn and small triangle of grass R then shortly, at next T-j in Hutton-le-Hole L 'Kirkbymoorside 3½, Malton 14'

19 Climb out of Hutton-le-Hole. **Easy to miss**. After 5 km (3 miles), at the end of descent, shortly after Keldholme Sawmill to the left, 1st R 'Keldholme only'

20 At T-j with A170 R onto tarmac path parallel with main road, then 1st R onto Old Road. Follow this back to the start

7 At T-j at the top of very steep climb L 'Castleton 6½'

8 After 5 km (3 miles), at summit of hill ignore right turn to Rosedale Abbey. Shortly take the next L 'Westerdale 2½'

9 *Easy to miss*. Fast descent over 4 km (2½ miles) into Westerdale. Towards the end of the village turn R by long, yellow stone cottage 'Castleton 2, Guisborough 11, Whitby 19'

10 At X-roads after 3 km (2 miles) R 'Castleton ½'. Short, steep climb

11 At T-j by triangle of grass on the edge of Castleton L 'Danby 2, Guisborough 9½, Whitby 17½'

12 At X-roads in Danby by the Duke of Wellington PH SA 'Leaholm 4, Moors Centre ½' (**For** on-road Route 4 turn L after Moors Centre)

13 Past the Moors Centre, under the railway bridge, then on sharp LH bend 1st R. Over humpbacked bridge and immediately L

14 At T-j near the castle ruins L

▼ *The Moors near Castleton*

15 After 2 km (1½ miles) and shortly after Crossley Side Farm 1st R steeply uphill 'Single track road'

16 After 5 km (3 miles) at T-j at the summit L 'Rosedale 3, Pickering 13' (**Or** for an easier return to the start, avoiding 2nd tough climb, turn R here 'Castleton 6' and follow signs for Hutton-le-Hole)

◀ page 33

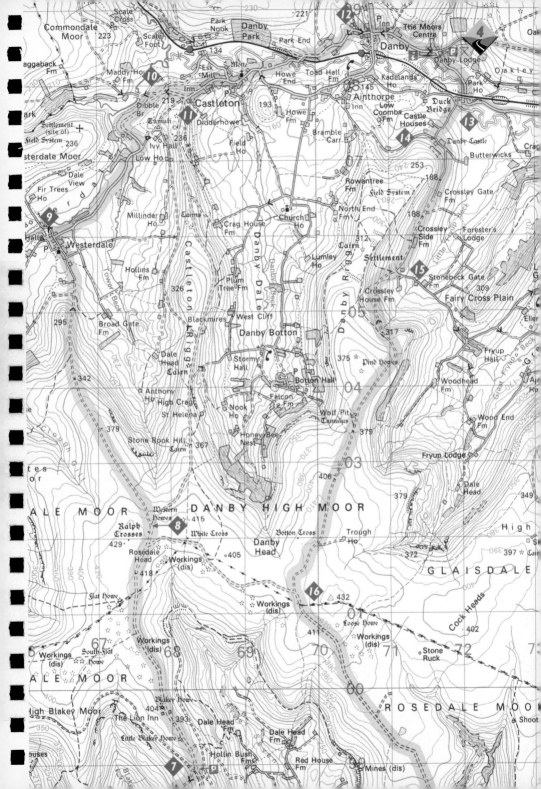

4 *West along the Esk Valley from Whitby*

*T*he best line along the valley floor of the River Esk is already taken up by the railway; this means that this valley route is anything but an easy outing as one short, steep climb follows the next long one. It is, however, a very beautiful and ultimately rewarding ride which almost entirely avoids busy roads. The pattern of the ride is set right from the start: a climb out of Whitby then a descent back down into the valley at Ruswarp. This roller-coaster style is followed through Sleights, Grosmont and Glaisdale as the ride crosses and re-crosses the river and railway line passing through lovely woodland. There is a relatively level section which leads to the Moors Centre at Danby. After this half-way point the climbs are fewer but longer. The first takes you to the highest point of the ride with views back down into Esk Dale. Beyond Ugthorpe everything is done to avoid the traffic – hence the circuitous up-and-down route into stream valleys, up through woodland and past outlying farmsteads. The gastronomic delights of Whitby can now be explored with a clear conscience!

Start

Tourist Information Centre, Whitby

P Cheapest long stay parking on Church Street on east side of River Esk or plenty of free parking just beyond instruction 3

20 Distance and grade

56 km (35 miles)

///// Strenuous

Terrain

Steep, wooded river and stream valleys to the north and south of Esk Dale. Total height gain – 1010 m (3315 ft)

Nearest railway

Whitby

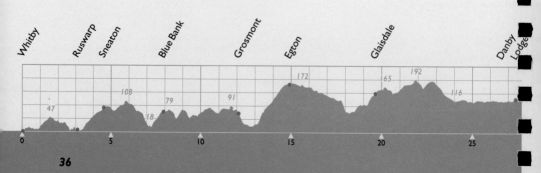

Refreshments

Plenty of choice in **Whitby**
Bridge PH 🍴, **Ruswarp**
Wilson Arms PH 🍴, **Beacon**
Farm tea shop, **Sneaton**
Plough Inn 🍴, **Sleights**
Station Tavern PH, tea room,
Grosmont
Horseshoe PH 🍴,
Wheatsheaf PH, **Egton**
Horse Shoe PH 🍴🍴, **Egton**
Bridge (just off the route)
Glaisdale Station tea rooms,
Arncliffe Arms PH, Mitre Tavern,
PH, **Glaisdale**
Wellington Arms PH, tea rooms
at Moors Centre, **Danby**
Black Bull Inn, **Ugthorpe**
Ye Olde Beehive, **Newholm**

▼ Colourful boats in
Whitby Harbour

Whitby 1
Former whaling port set on the Esk
Estuary. The Cook Museum recalls
the life and times of the explorer
Captain James Cook, who lived here
1746–49. St Mary's Church, at the top
of 199 steps, has an 18th-century
interior carved by ship-builders. The
sandstone ruins of Whitby Abbey are
on the cliff above the port

Grosmont 8
The hillside village is the northern ter-
minus for the North Yorkshire Moors
Railway. The sheds contain an exhibition
of steam engines and carriages dating
back to 1890. There is a 5-km (3-mile)
historical railway trail to Goathland

Glaisdale 9
An iron-smelting centre until ore
reserves ran out in the 1880s. The single-
arched packhorse bridge retains its
cobbles. A worn stone records the date,
1619, and 'TF' for Thomas Ferries. This
farmer's son fell in love with Agnes
Richardson, daughter of a rich landowner
who gave consent to the marriage only
on condition that Thomas became
wealthy. Ferries went straight to sea,
fought against the Armada, joined Drake
in piracy around the West Indies and did
become rich, returning to England and
Glaisdale some 6 years later

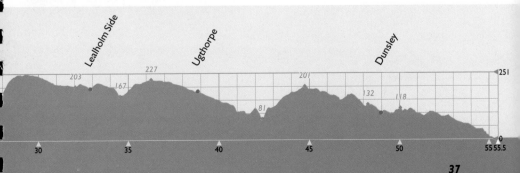

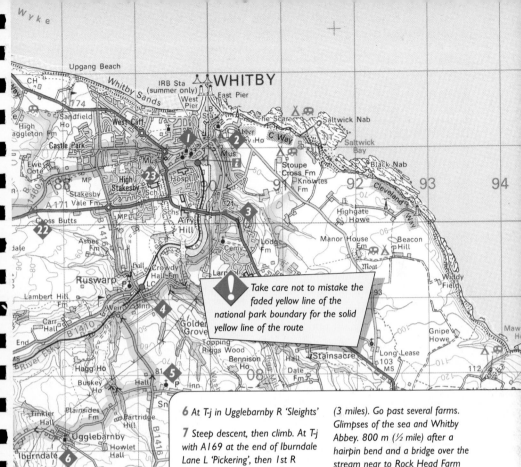

Take care not to mistake the faded yellow line of the national park boundary for the solid yellow line of the route

1 With back to the Tourist Information Centre in Whitby R, then at roundabout R towards the bridge

2 At traffic lights R, cross the bridge and follow road round to the R

3 At X-roads with A171 SA uphill towards Oak Tree Inn

4 At T-j with B1416 by bridge bear L (in effect SA). Busy road

5 After steep climb 1st R in Sneaton 'Ugglebarnby'

6 At T-j in Ugglebarnby R 'Sleights'

7 Steep descent, then climb. At T-j with A169 at the end of Iburndale Lane L 'Pickering', then 1st R 'Grosmont 2¾, Egton 4¼'

8 Through Grosmont, climb out of valley. At T-j in Egton R 'Whitby 7, Guisborough 16½', then L 'Glaisdale 2'

➥ **page 40**

16 Through Ugthorpe. After 3 km (2 miles) at X-roads at the bottom of hill by ford R 'Hutton Mulgrave 2'

17 After steep descent and very steep climb through wood, on a sharp RH bend shortly after Espsyke Farm on the left, bear 1st L (in effect SA)

18 Follow this lane for 5 km

(3 miles). Go past several farms. Glimpses of the sea and Whitby Abbey. 800 m (½ mile) after a hairpin bend and a bridge over the stream near to Rock Head Farm next L 'Sandsend, Dunsley'

19 After just over 1 km 1st R by farm and Dunsley Hall 'Newholm 1½, Whitby 4', then shortly at T-j R

20 At T-j L 'Newholm ½, Sandsend 2½'

21 Through Newholm. On sharp LH bend 1st R

22 At T-j (with B1460) L

23 At roundabout with A174 R 'Whitby Abbey, Scarborough' onto Chubb Hill Road, then at T-j L 'Town Centre' to return to the start

8 Through Grosmont, climb out of valley. At T-j in Egton R 'Whitby 7, Guisborough 16½', then L 'Glaisdale 2'

9 Descend to recross River Esk. Climb into Glaisdale. Follow signs for Leaholm through Glaisdale. Just over 1 km after Glaisdale, shortly after a dip, turn L by triangle of grass 'Fryup 3'

10 At X-roads SA (your ROW). Ignore a turn to the right and to the left. Shortly after descending to cross a small stream next R 'Houlsyke 1, Danby 2¾, Castleton 4¼'

11 At T-j L 'Danby 2, Danby Moors Centre 2' (**For** on-road Route 3 turn L over Duck Bridge)

12 Past the Moors Centre, then 1st R 'Danby Beacon 1½'. Steep climb. Fine valley views

13 At T-j after 5 km (3½ miles) L 'Ugthorpe, Whitby 9'

14 **Easy to miss.** After 1 km, just before a 'Bends, 16% hill' signpost turn L 'Guisborough 15' (i.e. **not** straight ahead signposted 'Whitby')

15 At T-j with A171 L 'Teeside', then after 800 m (½ mile)

(ignoring turn to Ugthorpe Caravan Park) 1st R 'Ugthorpe 1, Lythe 4'

16 Through Ugthorpe. After 3 km (2 miles) at X-roads at the bottom of hill by ford R 'Hutton Mulgrave 2'

17 After steep descent and very steep climb through wood, on a sharp RH bend shortly after Espsyke Farm on the left, bear 1st L (in effect SA)

page 39

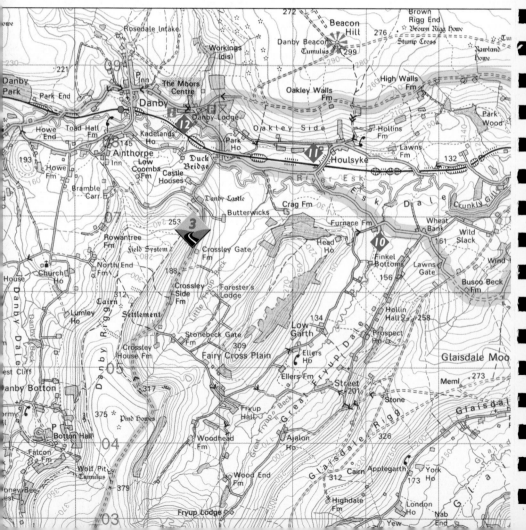

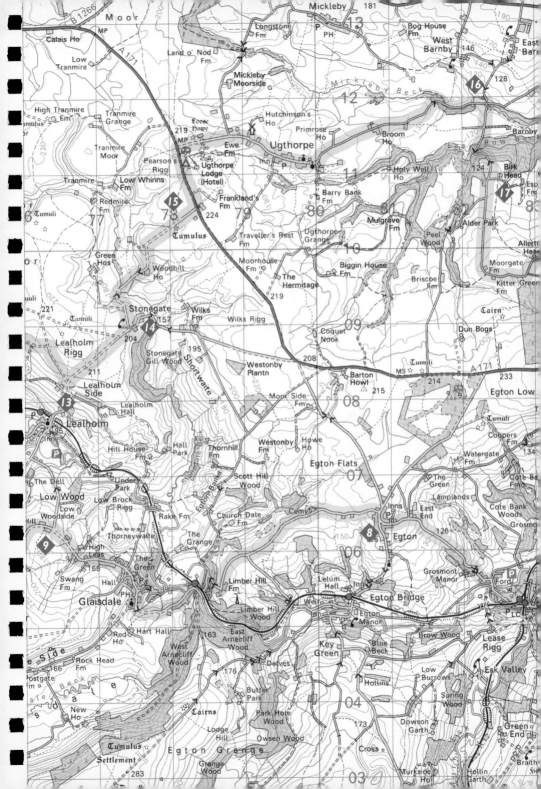

5 *From Thirsk, along the foot of the moors*

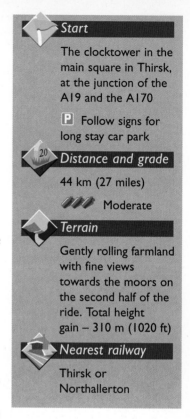

Start

The clocktower in the main square in Thirsk, at the junction of the A19 and the A170

🅿 Follow signs for long stay car park

Distance and grade

44 km (27 miles)

⚏⚏⚏ Moderate

Terrain

Gently rolling farmland with fine views towards the moors on the second half of the ride. Total height gain – 310 m (1020 ft)

Nearest railway

Thirsk or Northallerton

Like Helmsley, Thirsk has a large, open square that is used for weekly markets. Around the square stand fine old buildings and inns. The ride starting from Thirsk is broken into two halves: the first section runs parallel to the River Swale across land that rarely rises above 40 m (130 ft). At the crossroads with the A684 you have the option of creating a longer ride by missing out busy Northallerton and linking with on-road Route 1 at Yafforth then rejoining this ride at Bullamoor. The second half of the ride, in contrast, climbs through hills and woodland offering dramatic views of the moors just to the east. From Northallerton the ride soon climbs to over 90 m (300 ft). Once over Cod Beck the ride turns south parallel with the A19 and the escarpment of the North Yorkshire Moors, climbing to 152 m (500 ft) above Landmoth Wood. After passing beneath the A19 you climb to Upsall and the honeycomb stone in the walls, eroded by a mixture of wind and rain into some bizarre shapes. A final short and busy section on the A61 leads back to Thirsk.

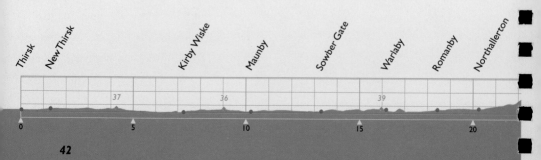

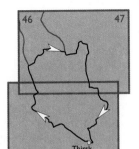

Thirsk I

As an important coaching station, Thirsk once boasted 35 pubs and four breweries – determined, it would seem, to send travellers merrily on their way. Many of these establishments still ply their trade, perhaps foremost among them is the Georgian Golden Fleece Inn, formerly the most important coaching inn, now the hub of the town on market days and race days. The vast square is still cobbled as it was when bull-baiting was held here in the 18th century. The Perpendicular church is the finest of its kind in the county. Begun in 1430, it was founded on a chantry built by Robert Thirsk, who died in 1419. He was a member of the ancient family which gave the town its name. Thirsk is also the birthplace of Thomas Lord (1755–1822), founder of Lord's Cricket Ground

▲ The Fleece, High Street Northallerton

Golden Fleece PH 🍺, plenty of choice in **Thirsk**
The Buck Inn, **Maunby**
Golden Lion PH 🍺, plenty of choice in **Northallerton**
Mill Garth Tea Rooms, near **Bullamoor**, east of **Northallerton**
Fox & Hounds PH, **Bullamoor**
Wheatsheaf Inn, **Borrowby**

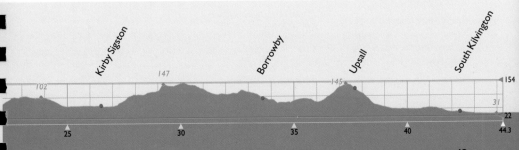

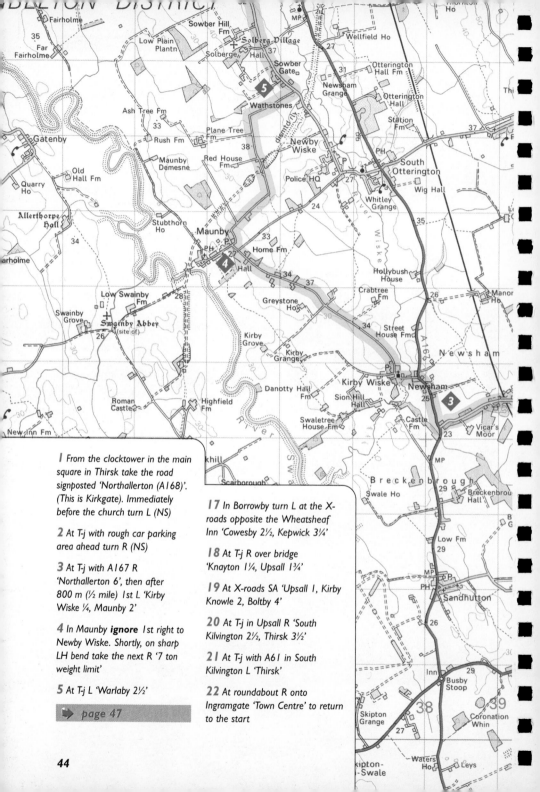

1 From the clocktower in the main square in Thirsk take the road signposted 'Northallerton (A168)'. (This is Kirkgate). Immediately before the church turn L (NS)

2 At T-j with rough car parking area ahead turn R (NS)

3 At T-j with A167 R 'Northallerton 6', then after 800 m (½ mile) 1st L 'Kirby Wiske ¼, Maunby 2'

4 In Maunby **ignore** 1st right to Newby Wiske. Shortly, on sharp LH bend take the next R '7 ton weight limit'

5 At T-j L 'Warlaby 2½'

➡ page 47

17 In Borrowby turn L at the X-roads opposite the Wheatsheaf Inn 'Cowesby 2½, Kepwick 3¼'

18 At T-j R over bridge 'Knayton 1¼, Upsall 1¾'

19 At X-roads SA 'Upsall 1, Kirby Knowle 2, Boltby 4'

20 At T-j in Upsall R 'South Kilvington 2½, Thirsk 3½'

21 At T-j with A61 in South Kilvington L 'Thirsk'

22 At roundabout R onto Ingramgate 'Town Centre' to return to the start

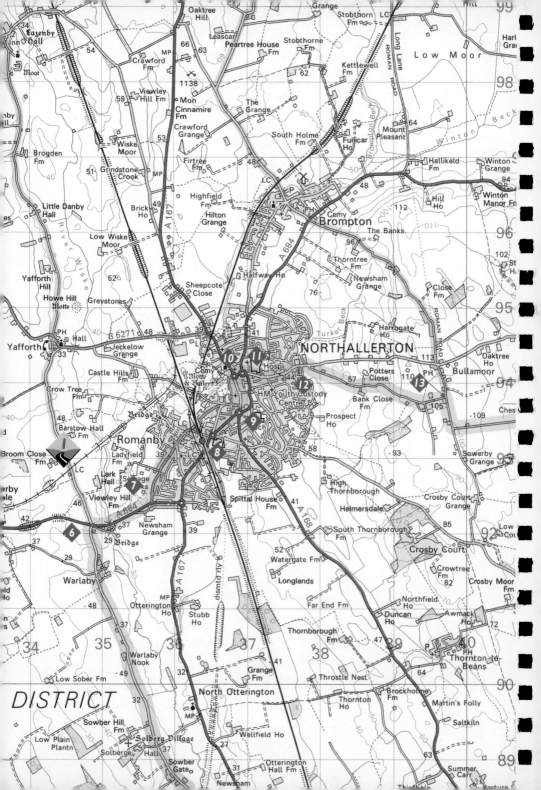

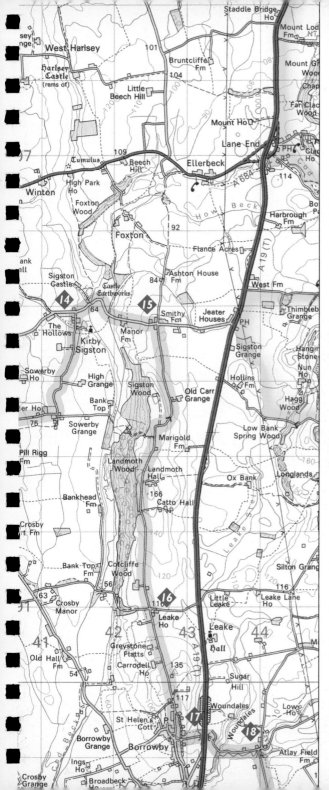

6 At X-roads with A684 R 'Romanby 1, Northallerton 2' (**Or** for longer ride, avoiding Northallerton, go SA 'Yafforth 1½', follow on-road Route 1 between instructions 3 and 13, then rejoin this route at instruction 13, below)

7 Take care – busy road. After 800 m (½ mile) 1st L onto Ainderby Road 'Romanby B1333'

8 Over railway lines and under bridge. **Follow carefully** – five roundabouts ahead! At 1st round-about at the end of Mill Lane 2nd exit onto South Parade 'A167 Town Centre'

9 At 2nd roundabout L 'Town Centre'

10 At 3rd roundabout, at the end of the High Street, R 'Civic Centre, Hambleton Leisure Centre'

11 At 4th roundabout bear R 'Thirsk A167', then at 5th round-about SA onto Bullamoor Road 'Community Centre, Craft Centre'

12 Easy to miss. Towards the edge of Northallerton, just past the school, ignore Ashlands Road to the right, take the next R 'Scholla Lane'

13 At T-j by triangle of grass R, then 1st L 'Sowerby under Cotcliffe ¾'

14 At T-j R 'Jeater Houses 1½, Osmotherley 4¼'

15 After just over 1 km 1st R at X-roads at the top of climb 'Borrowby 3'

16 After 4 km (2½ miles) at X-roads SA 'Borrowby 1'

17 In Borrowby turn L at the X-roads opposite the Wheatsheaf Inn 'Cowesby 2½, Kepwick 3¼'

18 At T-j R over bridge 'Knayton 1¼, Upsall 1¾'

◀ page 44

6 *Old abbeys and steep climbs west of Helmsley*

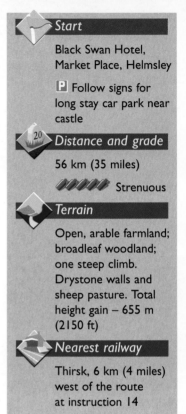

Start

Black Swan Hotel, Market Place, Helmsley

P Follow signs for long stay car park near castle

Distance and grade

56 km (35 miles)

Strenuous

Terrain

Open, arable farmland; broadleaf woodland; one steep climb. Drystone walls and sheep pasture. Total height gain – 655 m (2150 ft)

Nearest railway

Thirsk, 6 km (4 miles) west of the route at instruction 14

From Helmsley, in order to avoid the busy A170, the route heads east before turning west passing through the attractive, stone-built villages of Harome and Nunnington. As the route climbs out of Rye Dale there are fine views back across the river towards the hills to the north. The ride continues climbing past Ampleforth College, then shortly after Wass and Byland Abbey follows a delightful, wooded section on a tiny lane carrying next-to-no traffic. After an unpleasant stretch on the busy A170 through Sutton-under-Whitestonecliffe, you have a little time to collect your thoughts before an assault on the west face of the Moors, climbing over 152 m (500 ft) in about 1 km up Sneck Yate Bank. Your exertions are rewarded with a long, steady descent over several kilometres through Old Byland down into Rievaulx and the extraordinary ruins of the abbey. A last short, steep climb takes you up onto the B1257 and a final, long descent back to the start.

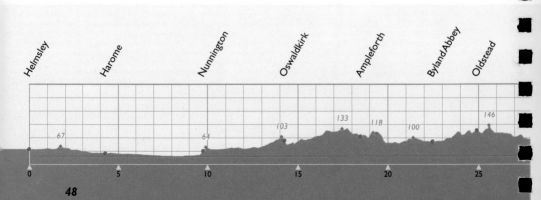

Places of interest

Helmsley 1

The castle retains the original 11th-century earthworks with stone walls built at a later stage rising from them. There are terraces, temples and riverside walks at Duncombe Park, built in 1713

Nunnington 5

Nunnington Hall features a Jacobean façade, a miniature, period room collection and a 17th-century walled garden

Byland Abbey 9

The remains of a 12th-century Cistercian monastery; the west front of the church still stands

Kilburn 11

Once home to the woodcarver Robert Thompson (died 1955) famous for the mouse trademark on his carvings. His workshop still functions

Refreshments

Feathers PH 🍴🍴, plenty of choice in **Helmsley**
Star PH 🍴🍴, **Harome**
Royal Oak PH 🍴🍴, **Nunnington**
Malt Shovel PH 🍴, **Oswaldkirk**
White Horse PH, White
Swan PH 🍴, **Ampleforth**
Wombwell Arms PH 🍴🍴, **Wass**
Abbey Inn 🍴🍴, **Byland Abbey**
Black Swan PH 🍴, **Oldstead**
Forresters Arms PH, Singing Bird Tea Room, **Kilburn**
Whitestonecliffe PH 🍴, **Sutton-under-Whitestonecliffe**

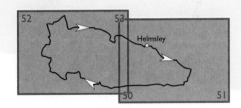

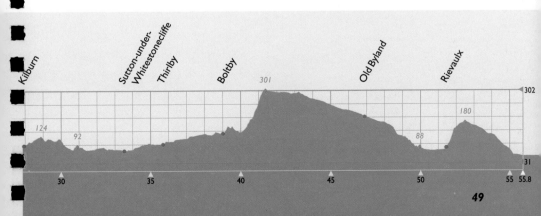

49

Take care not to mistake the faded yellow line of the national park boundary for the solid yellow line of the route

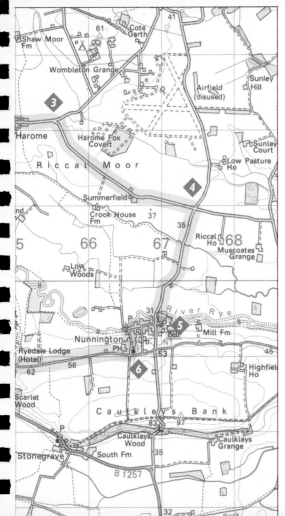

▲ *Roulston Scar from Sutton Bank*

1 With back to the Black Swan Hotel in the Market Place, Helmsley turn L on the A170 'Scarborough'.

2 Ignore right turn (Riccal Drive) at the end of the village. Use the tarmac path parallel with the main road. Take the next R 'Harome 2'

3 Follow signs for Wombleton and Nunnington through Harome. 800 m (½ mile) after the end of the village 1st R 'Nunnington 2½, Malton 13'

4 At X-roads by Give Way sign R 'Nunnington 1, Malton 11½'

5 Cross bridge by Nunnington Hall, then immediately R

6 At T-j by church at the top of the hill R

7 At T-j with B1257 R 'Helmsley 4'

8 Busy road. Climb steadily for about 1 km. 1st L onto B1363 'York 20½, Oswaldkirk ¼', Easingwold 10' then shortly, on sharp LH bend, bear R (in effect SA) 'Ampleforth 2½, Coxwold 7'

➡ **page 52**

21 Steep climb. At T-j with B1257 R 'Helmsley 2'. In Helmsley, 1st L immediately after church 'Kirkbymoorside, Scarborough'

51

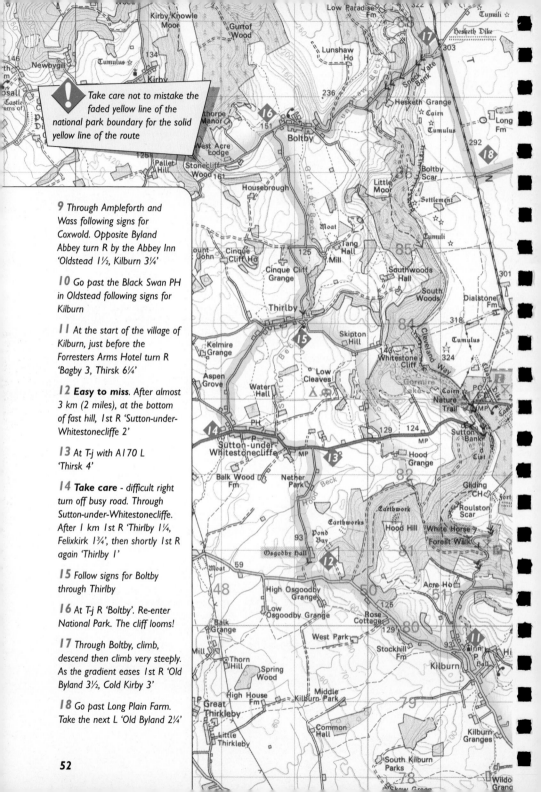

! Take care not to mistake the faded yellow line of the national park boundary for the solid yellow line of the route

9 Through Ampleforth and Wass following signs for Coxwold. Opposite Byland Abbey turn R by the Abbey Inn 'Oldstead 1½, Kilburn 3¼'

10 Go past the Black Swan PH in Oldstead following signs for Kilburn

11 At the start of the village of Kilburn, just before the Forresters Arms Hotel turn R 'Bagby 3, Thirsk 6¼'

12 Easy to miss. After almost 3 km (2 miles), at the bottom of fast hill, 1st R 'Sutton-under-Whitestonecliffe 2'

13 At T-j with A170 L 'Thirsk 4'

14 Take care - difficult right turn off busy road. Through Sutton-under-Whitestoncliffe. After 1 km 1st R 'Thirlby 1¼, Felixkirk 1¾', then shortly 1st R again 'Thirlby 1'

15 Follow signs for Boltby through Thirlby

16 At T-j R 'Boltby'. Re-enter National Park. The cliff looms!

17 Through Boltby, climb, descend then climb very steeply. As the gradient eases 1st R 'Old Byland 3½, Cold Kirby 3'

18 Go past Long Plain Farm. Take the next L 'Old Byland 2¼'

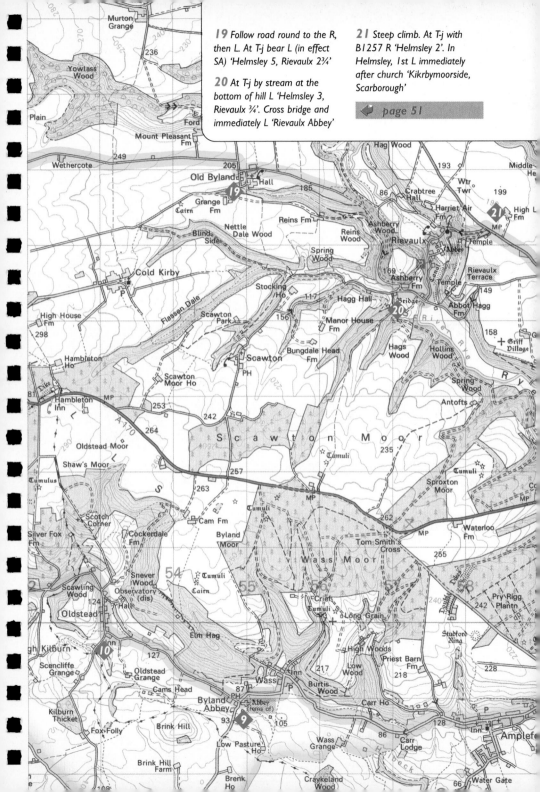

19 Follow road round to the R, then L. At T-j bear L (in effect SA) 'Helmsley 5, Rievaulx 2¾'

20 At T-j by stream at the bottom of hill L 'Helmsley 3, Rievaulx ¾'. Cross bridge and immediately L 'Rievaulx Abbey'

21 Steep climb. At T-j with B1257 R 'Helmsley 2'. In Helmsley, 1st L immediately after church 'Kikrbymoorside, Scarborough'

page 51

Helmsley, Kirkbymoorside and Bransdale

Helmsley and Kirkbymoorside are two of the most attractive towns of the North Yorkshire Moors. The ride starts from Helmsley, avoiding the busy A170 by dipping south through the fertile, arable land around Harome and Wombleton (watch out for Wimbles). A tarmac path parallel to the main road near to Kirkbymoorside means that the A170 is avoided altogether. Once beyond the fine stone buildings of Kirkbymoorside the road climbs to over 300 m (1000 ft) on its way north across the heather-clad hills lying to the east of Bransdale. The ride reaches its northernmost point at Bransdale Lodge, turns south then climbs to its highest point at 366 m (1200 ft) on the western slopes of Bransdale. Two further streams are crossed: one involving a short climb out of Bonfield Ghyll during the course of a long and wonderful descent; the second a much longer climb through the woodland above Riccal Dale to set you up for the final descent down into Helmsley.

Start

Black Swan Hotel, Market Place, Helmsley (on the A170 between Thirsk and Pickering)

P Follow signs

Distance and grade

45 km (28 miles)

Moderate/strenuous

Terrain

Flat, arable land between Helmsley and Kirkbymoorside. Heather moors around Bransdale. Total height gain – 660 m (2165 ft)

Nearest railway

Norton, 21 km (13 miles) southeast of the route at Kirkbymoorside

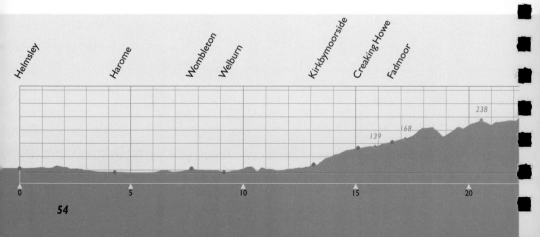

Helmsley 1

Much of the imposing semi-ruin of Helmsley Castle dates from the 12th and 13th centuries, including the 13th-century barbican (fortified gate). The massive keep was added to in the 14th century and there are fine Tudor domestic buildings which were in use until the early 18th century. Duncombe Park, just south of the town, is a splendid 18th-century house built in the style of the Restoration playwright-architect Sir John Vanbrugh (1664–1726). The magnificent grounds, including terraces, temples and riverside walks, were mostly laid out in the mid-18th century

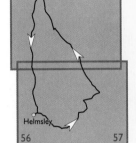

Kirk Dale 6

The wooded valley of Kirk Dale ('valley of the church') takes its name from the little St Gregory's Minster, a late Saxon Church with many details unaltered. Kirk Dale Cave, discovered in 1821, contained the bones of many Ice Age animals including hyenas, rhinoceroses, bison and hippopotamuses. The cave can be seen between the limestone beds high up in the quarry face across Hodge Beck

Refreshments

Feathers PH 🍴🍷, *plenty of choice in* **Helmsley**
Star PH 🍴🍷, Pheasant PH, **Harome**
Plough PH, **Wombleton**
George & Dragon PH 🍴🍷, *plenty of choice in* **Kirkbymoorside**
Plough Inn, **Fadmoor**

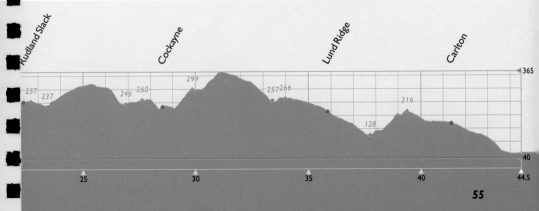

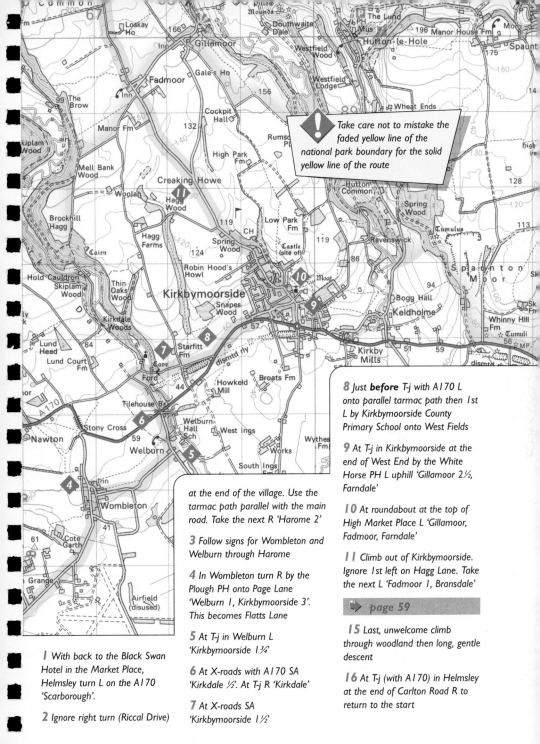

! Take care not to mistake the faded yellow line of the national park boundary for the solid yellow line of the route

at the end of the village. Use the tarmac path parallel with the main road. Take the next R 'Harome 2'

3 Follow signs for Wombleton and Welburn through Harome

4 In Wombleton turn R by the Plough PH onto Page Lane 'Welburn 1, Kirkbymoorside 3'. This becomes Flatts Lane

5 At T-j in Welburn L 'Kirkbymoorside 1¾'

6 At X-roads with A170 SA 'Kirkdale ½'. At T-j R 'Kirkdale'

7 At X-roads SA 'Kirkbymoorside 1½'

1 With back to the Black Swan Hotel in the Market Place, Helmsley turn L on the A170 'Scarborough'.

2 Ignore right turn (Riccal Drive)

8 Just **before** T-j with A170 L onto parallel tarmac path then 1st L by Kirkbymoorside County Primary School onto West Fields

9 At T-j in Kirkbymoorside at the end of West End by the White Horse PH L uphill 'Gillamoor 2½, Farndale'

10 At roundabout at the top of High Market Place L 'Gillamoor, Fadmoor, Farndale'

11 Climb out of Kirkbymoorside. Ignore 1st left on Hagg Lane. Take the next L 'Fadmoor 1, Bransdale'

⮑ page 59

15 Last, unwelcome climb through woodland then long, gentle descent

16 At T-j (with A170) in Helmsley at the end of Carlton Road R to return to the start

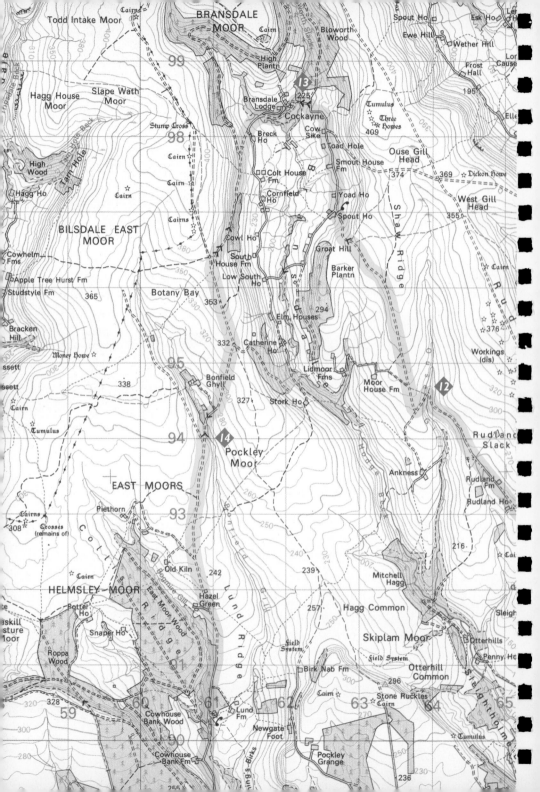

12 Through Fadmoor following signs for Bransdale

13 After 6 km (4 miles) drop into, then climb out of valley of Ouse Gill

14 After further 5 km (3½ miles) (and 2 km (1½ miles) after passing telephone box) drop steeply to cross stream of Bloworth Slack. Shortly, turn L 'Helmsley 10'

14 Climb for 2 km (1½ miles), then (with one short dip) lovely descent over 6 km (4 miles)

◀ page 57

▲ The edge of the moorland beneath Rudland Rigg

8 ◆ Through the Langdale and Dalby Forests

Start

New Inn, Thornton-le-Dale, 5 km (3 miles) east of Pickering

P Large car park signed off the road towards Malton

Distance and grade

56 km (35 miles)

Moderate/strenuous

Terrain

Flat arable land at the start. Hills and forestry after Snainton. Total height gain – 630 m (2070 ft)

Nearest railway

Norton, 7 km (4 miles) from the route at instruction 3

As with on-road Route 9, this route moves from the richly cultivated lowlands into the hills. The first 8 km (5 miles) are unavoidably on roads carrying more traffic than is ideal for leisure cycling but a turn off the A169, towards Low Marishes, takes you onto a quiet lane for a further 11 km (7 miles). After Snainton the ride climbs up away from the flat lands and the hedges are increasingly replaced by drystone walls. After the first summit the route becomes a roller-coaster of descents and climbs, in and out of the valleys formed by Troutsdale Beck and the River Derwent. The Forest Drive (free for cyclists) starts soon after Bickley and is followed through conifer plantations and clearings, climbing to over 244 m (800 ft) then descending alongside Staindale Beck and Dalby Beck to Low Dalby. Just when you thought it was one long, downhill run back to Thornton-le-Dale, you are faced with the final climb of the day – 60 m (200 ft). This sets you up for the fast drop back down to the start.

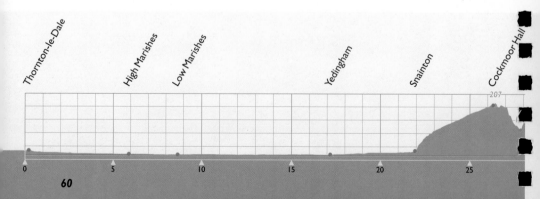

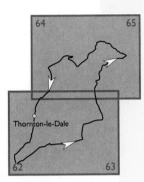

64 65

Thornton-le-Dale

62 63

Places of interest

Thornton-le-Dale 1
The village has a variety of architecture: buildings include 12 darkstone almshouses built in 1656, a Tudor thatched cottage, Georgian mansions and a medieval church

Snainton 5/6
Mile Bush Open Farm illustrates the region's agricultural past with various animals and old implements as part of a working farm

Troutsdale 6-8
From the River Derwent the road leads up the steep valley of Troutsdale Beck with Wykeham Forest to the east. At the summit of the climb the moors fall away in a series of flat plateaux

Refreshments

New Inn, Buck Inn, tea rooms, **Thornton-le-Dale** School House Inn, **Low Marishes** Foxholmes Inn, **Ebberston** (just off the route between 3 and 4) Coachman Inn, Peacock Inn, **Snainton** Tea room at **Milebush Farm**, north of **Snainton** Moorcock Inn 🍴, **Langdale End** Jingleby Farm tea room, on the forest drive

▲ Bridestonre, Dalby Forest

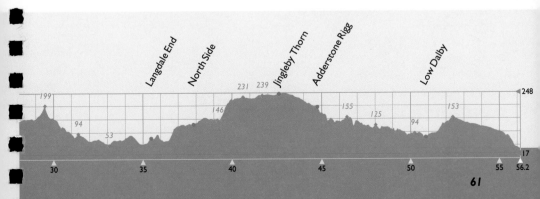

Take care not to mistake the faded yellow line of the national park boundary for the solid yellow line of the route

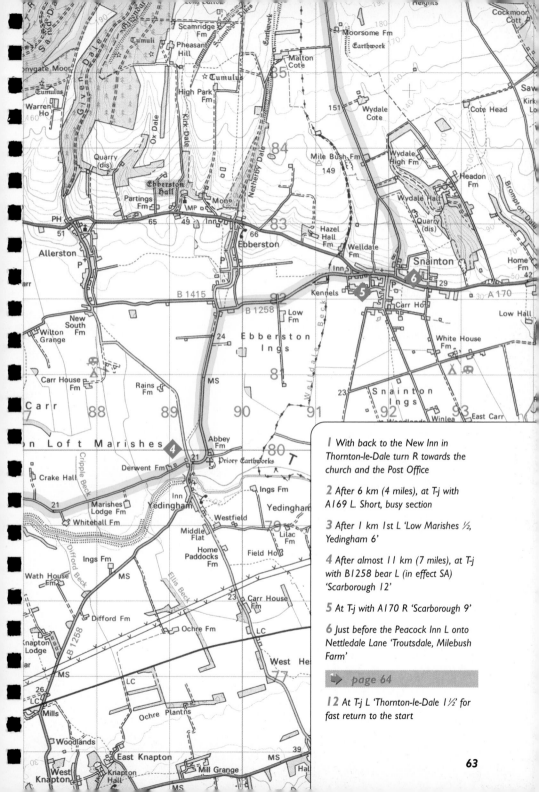

1 With back to the New Inn in Thornton-le-Dale turn R towards the church and the Post Office

2 After 6 km (4 miles), at T-j with A169 L. Short, busy section

3 After 1 km 1st L 'Low Marishes ½, Yedingham 6'

4 After almost 11 km (7 miles), at T-j with B1258 bear L (in effect SA) 'Scarborough 12'

5 At T-j with A170 R 'Scarborough 9'

6 Just before the Peacock Inn L onto Nettledale Lane 'Troutsdale, Milebush Farm'

➡ page 64

12 At T-j L 'Thornton-le-Dale 1½' for fast return to the start

7 Steep then steady climb over 5 km (3 miles). After start of descent, follow road sharply round to the R 'Troutsdale, Hackness 5'

8 Descend, climb then descend again to cross River Derwent. Climb to T-j and turn L sharply back on yourself 'Broxa, Langdale End'

9 Recross river, through Langdale End and follow signs for Bickley and Dalby End through toll gate

10 Follow the Forest Drive for 18 km (11 miles), climbing to 248 m (815 ft), then descending to 90 m (300 ft) at Low Dalby and Information Centre

11 Final climb of the ride beyond Dalby Beck

12 At T-j L 'Thornton-le-Dale 1½' for fast return to the start

◀ page 63

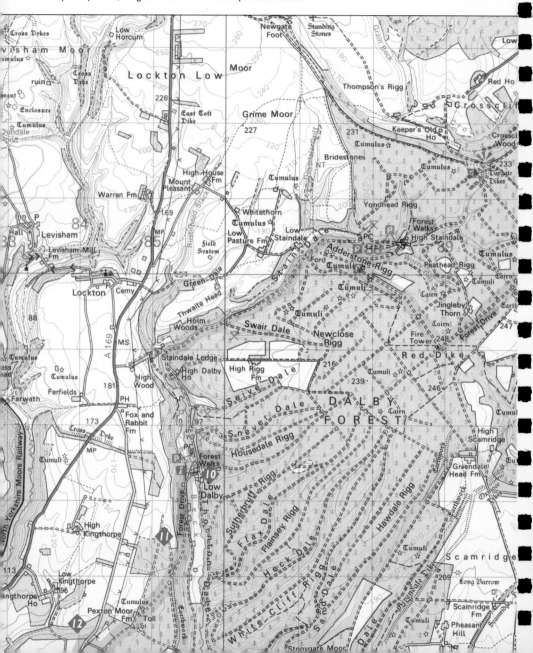

Take care not to mistake the faded yellow line of the national park boundary for the solid yellow line of the route

9 From Malton to the foothills of the moors

This is a long ride to the north of Malton but there are plenty of opportunities of making it shorter and easier by cutting out the climb from Pickering up onto the moors near Cropton. The route manages to escape from Malton on quiet roads and tracks, short sections of which are unsealed but should be passable in all but the worst weather. Shortly after crossing Costa Beck near Kirby Misperton a second track leads onto a delightful lane alongside a stream leading right into the heart of Pickering. Views open up behind you as you climb out of Pickering and the scenery changes to one of drystone walls, gorse and forestry. The route drops down through the pretty village of Cropton into the valley of the River Seven, climbs up to the wide street of stone-built houses in Appleton-le-Moors for the last wide-ranging views of the day before the crossing of the levels on the lovely network of lanes through Great Edstone, Brawby, Great Barugh and Great Habton. The return and the outward route link at Ryton, 5 km (3 miles) from the start.

Start

Tourist Information Centre, Market Place, Malton

P Follow signs for long stay car parks near the railway station

Distance and grade

61 km (38 miles)

Moderate

Terrain

Flat arable country between Malton and Pickering. Forestry and moorland to the north of Pickering. Total height gain – 375 m (1230 ft)

Nearest railway

Norton

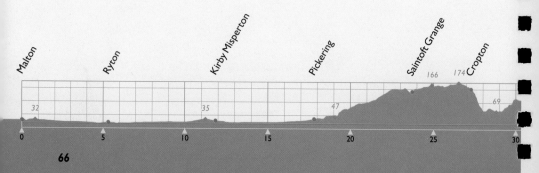

Malton 1

The old market town surrounds a church dating from Norman times. The museum tells the town's history from 8000 BC – included are the Roman fort remains from AD 70. Stone houses dating from the 18th-century line the main street

Eden Camp 3/4

A former POW camp houses a vivid re-creation of the World War II era of British life. The sights, sounds and smells of enemy bombing raids, day-to-day life of rationing and propaganda are all portrayed

Pickering 9

Originally a Celtic town dating from the 3rd century BC, the castle has Norman remnants and the church has medieval frescoes and effigies. The Beck Isle Museum of Rural Life recalls the Victorian era with typical printer's shop, outfitters and cobblers

▼*Goathland Station*

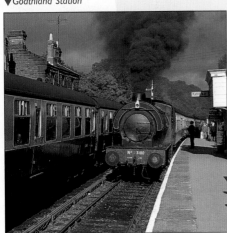

Refreshments

Plenty of choice in **Malton** Black Swan PH 🍴, Forest & Vale PH 🍴, plenty of choice in **Pickering** New Inn 🍴🍴, **Cropton** Appleton Hall Hotel, Moors Inn, **Appleton-le-Moors** Grey Horse Inn, **Great Edstone** Golden Lion Inn, **Great Barugh** Grapes Inn, **Great Habton**

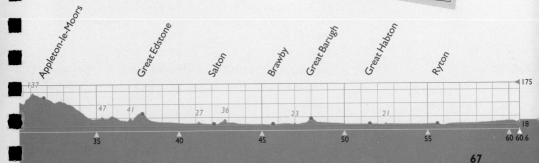

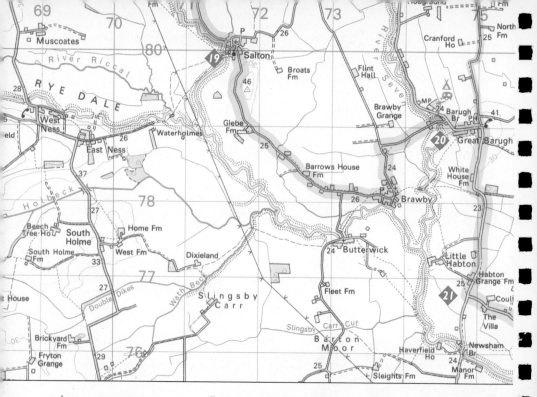

1 From the Tourist Information Centre in Market Place, Malton go R uphill onto Newgate, then 1st R onto Spital Street. At X-roads SA onto Princess Road

2 Shortly, on sharp RH bend with 'Pickering' signposted to the right bear L (in effect SA). At X-roads SA onto Rainbow Lane. At the end of the houses SA onto Public Bridleway (unsealed surface but passable)

3 At T-j L to cross bridge over the bypass

4 Second rough section. Take 2nd R onto tarmac lane. At T-j L

5 After 5 km (3½ miles) at T-j R 'Kirby Misperton 1¾, Pickering 6'

6 At roundabout at the end of Main Street in Kirby Misperton R 'Pickering 4, Malton 7'

7 After 1 km and shortly after crossing humpbacked bridge 1st track L 'Lendales Farm, 15 mph speed limit'

8 Over bridge, go past farmhouse on the right, then follow track as it swings R, then L between farm buildings to rejoin tarmac lane

⇨ page 70

19 Through Salton following signs for Brawby and through Brawby following signs for Malton

20 At T-j, just over 1 km after Brawby, R 'Malton 6¾'. At T-j in Great Barugh after the Golden Lion Inn R 'Malton 6¼'

21 **Easy to miss**. After 3 km (1¾ miles) 1st L 'Great Habton ¾, Kirby Misperton 3¼'

22 After 1 km on sharp LH bend

by the Grapes Inn in Great Habton R 'Ryton 2½'

23 After 4 km (2½ miles) at T-j in Ryton R 'Malton 3'. Rejoin outward route

24 Cross bridge over River Rye. 1 km after the bridge and 180 m (200 yd) after passing farm buildings to the left and right take the next R 'Windmill Farm'

25 At T-j L onto track. Cross bridge over bypass, then 1st R just before the power lines

26 Through housing estate. At X-roads SA. At T-j R downhill onto Princess Road

27 At X-roads at the end of Princess Road by Give Way sign SA, then 1st L to return to the Tourist Information Centre

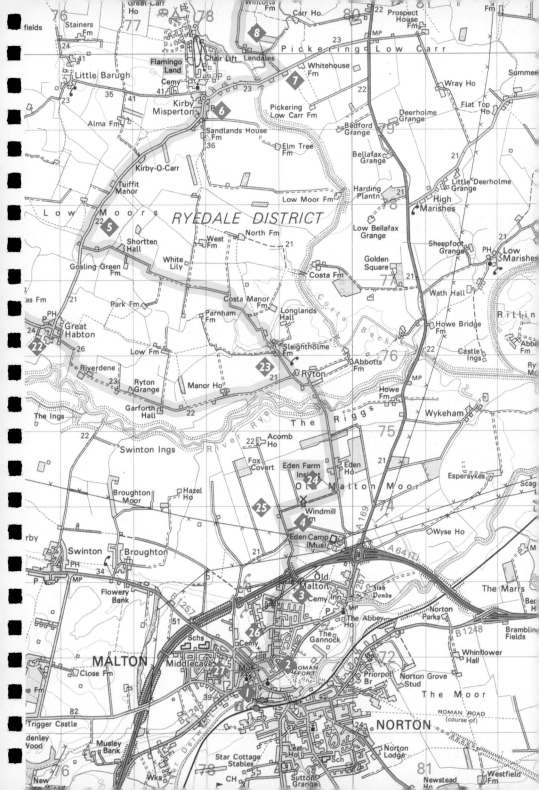

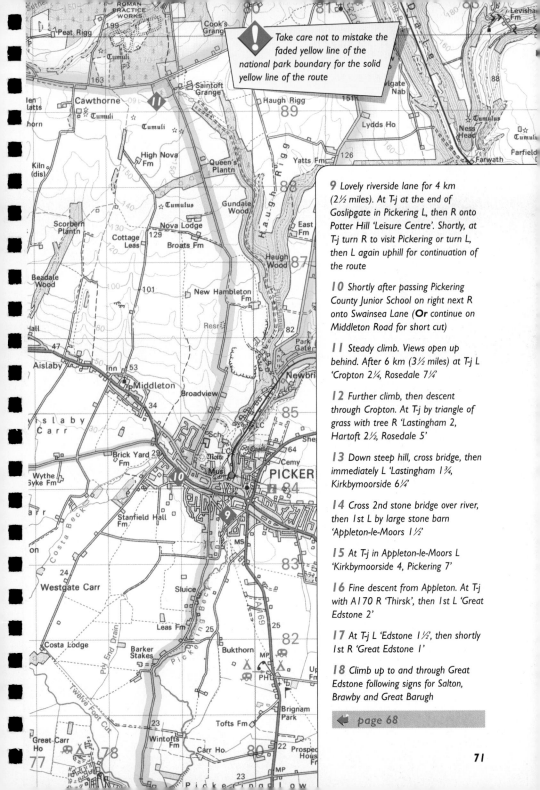

Take care not to mistake the faded yellow line of the national park boundary for the solid yellow line of the route

9 Lovely riverside lane for 4 km (2½ miles). At T-j at the end of Goslipgate in Pickering L, then R onto Potter Hill 'Leisure Centre'. Shortly, at T-j turn R to visit Pickering or turn L, then L again uphill for continuation of the route

10 Shortly after passing Pickering County Junior School on right next R onto Swainsea Lane (**Or** continue on Middleton Road for short cut)

11 Steady climb. Views open up behind. After 6 km (3½ miles) at T-j L 'Cropton 2¼, Rosedale 7¼'

12 Further climb, then descent through Cropton. At T-j by triangle of grass with tree R 'Lastingham 2, Hartoft 2½, Rosedale 5'

13 Down steep hill, cross bridge, then immediately L 'Lastingham 1¾, Kirkbymoorside 6¼'

14 Cross 2nd stone bridge over river, then 1st L by large stone barn 'Appleton-le-Moors 1½'

15 At T-j in Appleton-le-Moors L 'Kirkbymoorside 4, Pickering 7'

16 Fine descent from Appleton. At T-j with A170 R 'Thirsk', then 1st L 'Great Edstone 2'

17 At T-j L 'Edstone 1½', then shortly 1st R 'Great Edstone 1'

18 Climb up to and through Great Edstone following signs for Salton, Brawby and Great Barugh

10 South from Malton to Kirkham Priory and Thixendale

Malton is a fine base for exploring many of the rides in the region. Most of the roads leading out of the town carry quite a lot of traffic and it is not until climbing past the quarry on the Welham road and turning onto the minor lanes that you truly feel the ride has begun. These quiet lanes take you alongside the River Derwent, down past the delights of Kirkham Priory and briefly onto the west side of the Derwent Valley. From Howsham Bridge on the River Derwent the route climbs 219 m (720 ft) over 8 km (5 miles) before a long and glorious descent into Thixendale. The route continues its gentle descent for a further 3 km (2 miles) before a steep climb past the appropriately named Fairy Dale up onto Wharram Percy Wold. Rolling wold country is crossed over Duggleby Wold to South Wold before the ride strikes east through Settrington. In order to avoid the busy B1248, it is suggested that you use 800 m (½ mile) of stone-based bridleway to enter Norton on one of its quieter approach roads.

Start

Tourist Information Centre, Market Place, Malton

P Follow signs for long stay car park near the railway station

Distance and grade

52 km (32 miles)

Moderate/strenuous

Terrain

Valley of the River Derwent, wold hills and dales. Total height gain – 535 m (1755 ft)

Nearest railway

Norton

74   Malton   75

76   77

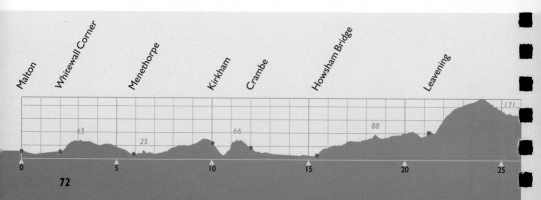

Malton · Whitewall Corner · Menethorpe · Kirkham · Crambe · Howsham Bridge · Leavening

171

65   66   88

25

0   5   10   15   20   25

Refreshments

Plenty of choice in **Malton/Norton**
Stone Trough PH 🍺🍴, **Kirkham**
Jolly Farmers PH, **Leavening**
Cross Keys PH 🍴, two tea rooms,
Thixendale
Red House tea room, **Wharram le Street**

Kirkham Priory 7
Augustinian Priory on the River Derwent, dating from the 12th century. It has a Norman doorway and a richly carved 13th-century gatehouse façade

Wharram Percy 13
A lost village, victim of a 15th-century landlord's decision to switch from arable to sheep farming. Only the church ruin remains

Duggleby Howe 14
A Stone Age mound where eight adults and two children were buried with their belongings. Finds include 4000-year-old tools made from the antlers of red deer

▲ Old stone bridge over the River Derwent near Kirkham Priory

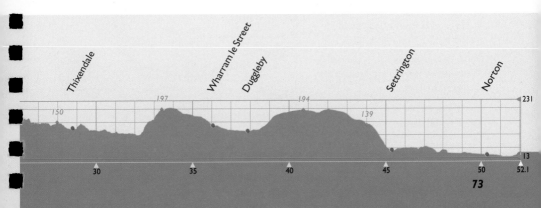

1 From the Tourist Information Centre in the Market Place, Malton turn R onto Finkle Street, then at T-j after 45 m (50 yd) R. At X-roads and traffic lights SA onto Castlegate 'Beverley B1248'

2 **Take care**. Difficult right turn – be prepared to pull in and wait for a gap in the traffic. Cross bridge over the River Derwent, then immediately R after railway crossing onto Welham Road 'Stamford Bridge 12, Pocklington 17'

3 Climb. Immediately after the quarry next R 'Menethorpe 1'

4 After (2½ miles) at T-j R 'Westow 1¼, Kirkham 2¼'

5 After 1 km on sharp LH bend by triangle of grass bear R 'Firby ½, Kirkham Abbey 1'

6 At T-j R 'Kirkham ¼, York 13' (or L for Stone Trough PH). Go slowly! Some of the best views of the abbey are at the top of the hill

7 Go past abbey, cross river, short, steep climb 1st L at X-roads 'Crambe ½'

8 After 2 km (1½ miles) SA at level crossing. At T-j L 'Howsham 1, Leavening 4'

9 After 3 km (2 miles) at X-roads by Give Way sign SA 'Leavening 1¾, Burythorpe 3, Thixendale 6'

10 Through Leavening. Steep then steady climb. At X-roads SA 'Thixendale 3, Burdale 5'

➥ page 77

17 After 2 km (1½ miles) at T-j with B1248 SA onto track 'Bridleway'. In deepest winter or after heavy rain the track will be muddy, so turn R and use (busy) B1248 to rejoin route at 2nd part of instruction 18

18 At T-j R. At mini-roundabout in Norton L. Immediately after the level crossing turn L onto Norton Road

19 At T-j at the end of Railway Street L, then immediately R onto Saville Street to return to Market Place

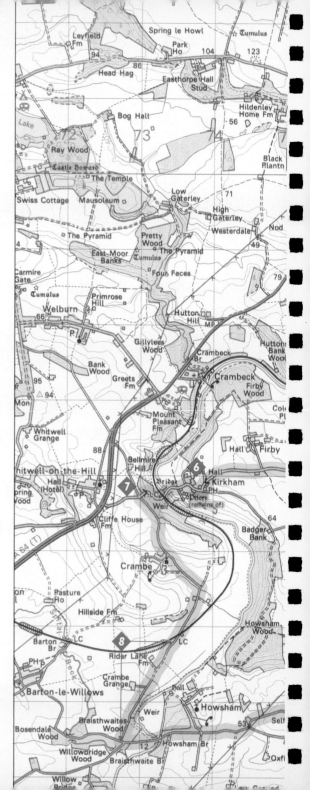

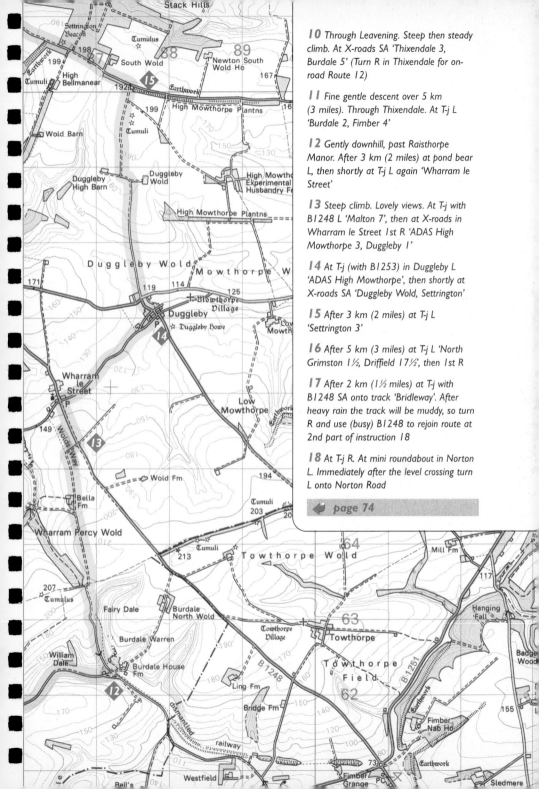

10 Through Leavening. Steep then steady climb. At X-roads SA 'Thixendale 3, Burdale 5' (Turn R in Thixendale for on-road Route 12)

11 Fine gentle descent over 5 km (3 miles). Through Thixendale. At T-j L 'Burdale 2, Fimber 4'

12 Gently downhill, past Raisthorpe Manor. After 3 km (2 miles) at pond bear L, then shortly at T-j L again 'Wharram le Street'

13 Steep climb. Lovely views. At T-j with B1248 L 'Malton 7', then at X-roads in Wharram le Street 1st R 'ADAS High Mowthorpe 3, Duggleby 1'

14 At T-j (with B1253) in Duggleby L 'ADAS High Mowthorpe', then shortly at X-roads SA 'Duggleby Wold, Settrington'

15 After 3 km (2 miles) at T-j L 'Settrington 3'

16 After 5 km (3 miles) at T-j L 'North Grimston 1½, Driffield 17½', then 1st R

17 After 2 km (1½ miles) at T-j with B1248 SA onto track 'Bridleway'. After heavy rain the track will be muddy, so turn R and use (busy) B1248 to rejoin route at 2nd part of instruction 18

18 At T-j R. At mini roundabout in Norton L. Immediately after the level crossing turn L onto Norton Road

page 74

Into the heart of wold country, south of Sherburn

A curious feature of the area is the plantations of trees around the farmhouses to protect them from the icy blast of the winds from the north and the northeast. This is a landscape scattered with outlying farms, woodland copses and small stone villages. A steep climb out of Sherburn takes you to the high point of the outward leg of the ride before a long descent to Foxholes. Two further climbs take you to Kilham, the largest village visited, with many attractive stone houses. The rolling ride continues west then north, climbing to a high point of 177 m (580 ft) above Sherburn which marks the start of the final descent. There are countless opportunities to extend the ride east towards Bridlington and Flamborough Head, southwest towards Pocklington or west towards Malton or indeed to shorten the route by cutting west from Foxholes on the road through Butterwick and Weaverthorpe.

Start

The crossroads in Sherburn, on the A64 between Malton and Scarborough

P No specific parking – use the main street heading north away from the A64

 Distance and grade

42 km (26 miles)

Moderate/strenuous

Terrain

Typical rolling wold country. Total height gain – 530 m (1740 ft)

Nearest railway

Hunmanby, 10 km (6 miles) northeast of Thwing

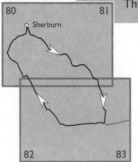

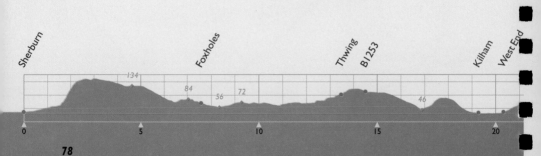

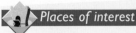

Places of interest

Rudston 5 km (3 miles) east of the route at 7
Britain's tallest standing stone, 7 m (25 ft) high and weighing 46 tons, stands in the churchyard of All Saints Church. It is a testament to the skill and faith of the Neolithic people who erected it

Burton Agnes 5 km (3 miles) southeast of the route at 8
A well-preserved, mainly Jacobean, house containing a picture collection with works by Utrillo, Gauguin, Cezanne and Matisse

Refreshments

East Riding PH, Pigeon Pie PH, **Sherburn**
Rampant Horse PH, **Thwing**
Bay Horse PH, **Kilham**

▼ Burton Agnes

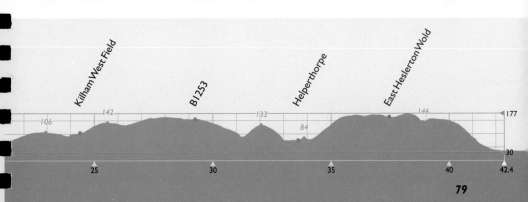

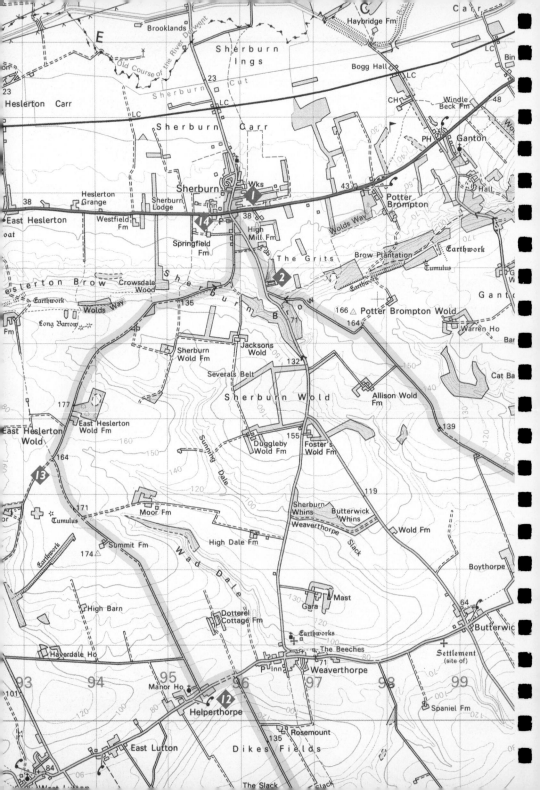

1 From the traffic lights at the end of St Hilda's Street in Sherburn go SA across the A64 onto minor lane

2 After 1 km 1st L immediately after Sherburn Pumping Station

3 Over next 6 km (4 miles) steep climb, then more gentle descent. At T-j R into Foxholes. At T-j with B1249 at the end of Ganton Road R 'Langtoft 5, Driffield 11', then 1st L by row of red brick houses

4 Follow the lane round to the R. At X-roads by Give Way sign SA

5 After just over 1 km, shortly after sharp LH and RH bends, next L opposite Octon Grange

6 At X-roads in Thwing R 'Driffield 9½, Kilham 4'

➡ **page 82**

12 At T-j at the bottom of the hill L 'Helperthorpe ¼, Malton 14', then 1st R 'East Heslerton Wold'

13 At T-j R 'Sherburn 2½'

14 At T-j at the bottom of the hill L to return to the start

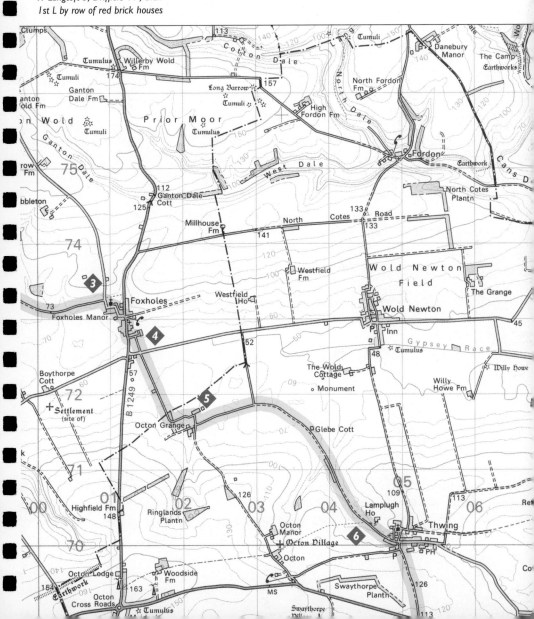

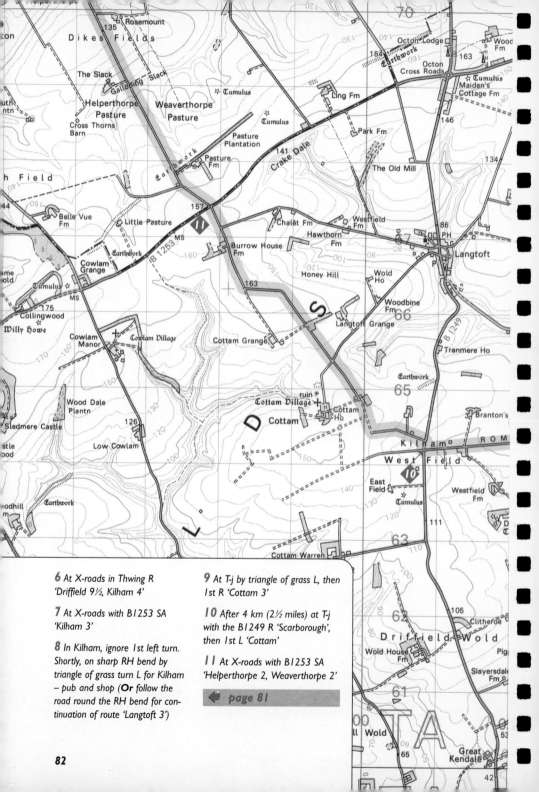

6 At X-roads in Thwing R 'Driffield 9½, Kilham 4'

7 At X-roads with B1253 SA 'Kilham 3'

8 In Kilham, ignore 1st left turn. Shortly, on sharp RH bend by triangle of grass turn L for Kilham – pub and shop (**Or** follow the road round the RH bend for continuation of route 'Langtoft 3')

9 At T-j by triangle of grass L, then 1st R 'Cottam 3'

10 After 4 km (2½ miles) at T-j with the B1249 R 'Scarborough', then 1st L 'Cottam'

11 At X-roads with B1253 SA 'Helperthorpe 2, Weaverthorpe 2'

◀ page 81

Thixendale and the heart of the Wolds, from Pocklington

12

Start

The Black Bull PH, Market Place, Pocklington

P Follow signs

Distance and grade

51 km (32 miles)

Moderate/ strenuous

Terrain

Rolling wold country, deepest valleys in the wolds, attractive villages. Total height gain – 480 m (1575 ft)

Nearest railway

Norton, 13 km (8 miles) north of the route at Thixendale or Driffield, 10 km (6 miles) northeast of the route at North Dalton

One of two rides starting from the attractive wolds town of Pocklington, both routes explore the highest hills and the deepest valleys of this gently rolling countryside; these provide some of the best cycling in the area covered by this book with easier gradients and less height gain than the tougher challenges of the Yorkshire Moors to the north. Like the other famous wold country of the Cotswolds, the area has a mixture of drystone walls and hedgerows, of arable and grazing land and attractive stone villages – most particularly Thixendale which nestles at the bottom of the valley. There have been two climbs so far, one short and steep up from Burnby and a longer steadier one from North Dalton onto Huggate Wold. The third and last climb of the day may well be the hardest after a plateful of cakes at the Thixendale tea rooms but is worth it for the thrilling descent that drops you back in Pocklington

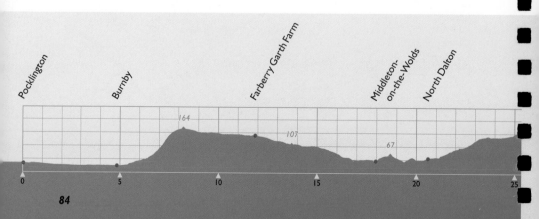

Places of interest

Pocklington 1
All Saints' Church in this attractive market town was built between 1200 and 1450 and has a 15th-century tower. Inside is the 14th-century churchyard cross. The Penny Arcadia houses a collection of amusement machines

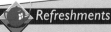

Refreshments

Feathers PH 🍴, plenty of choice in **Pocklington** Robin Hood Inn, **Middleton-on-the-Wolds** Star PH 🍴, Old School Tea Room, **North Dalton** Wolds Inn, **Huggate** Cross Keys PH 🍴, two tea rooms, **Thixendale**

▲ *Near Pocklington*

Burnby Hall 3
Over 50 water-lily varieties grow in the garden created around two lakes. In the rest of the grounds are roses, lilacs and Japanese maples

Londesborough *off the route near 3/4*
The estate was bought by a 19th-century railway magnate to foil a rival's rail scheme. He extended Londesborough Park in Baronial style

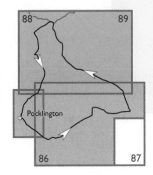

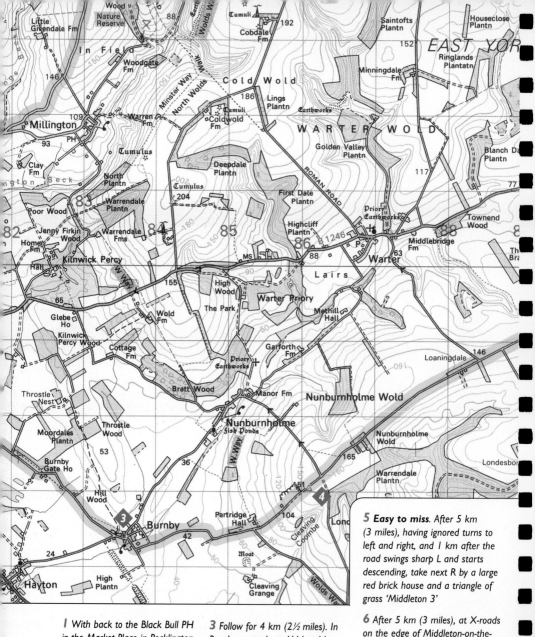

1 With back to the Black Bull PH in the Market Place in Pocklington L, then at T-j with Regent Street L again

2 At T-j with The Balk L, then after 275 m (300 yd) 1st proper road R 'Burnby 3'

3 Follow for 4 km (2½ miles). In Burnby, on a sharp LH bend by church turn R 'Londesborough 2½, Middleton 8'

4 At X-roads at the top of 130-m (425-ft) climb SA 'Middleton 6, North Dalton 7'

5 *Easy to miss. After 5 km (3 miles), having ignored turns to left and right, and 1 km after the road swings sharp L and starts descending, take next R by a large red brick house and a triangle of grass 'Middleton 3'*

6 After 5 km (3 miles), at X-roads on the edge of Middleton-on-the-Wolds L for continuation of route (**Or** R to visit Middleton)

7 At T-j with B2146 in North Dalton bear R (in effect SA) 'Driffield 7', then shortly after Star

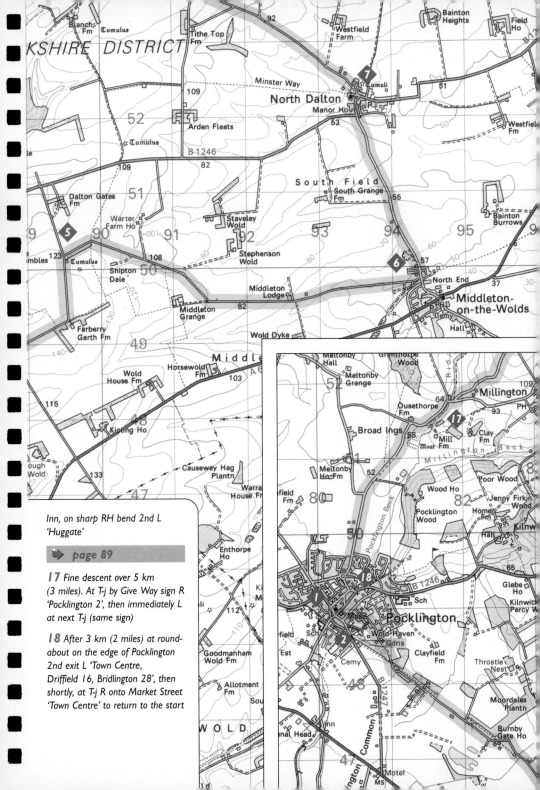

Inn, on sharp RH bend 2nd L
'Huggate'

➡ **page 89**

17 Fine descent over 5 km
(3 miles). At T-j by Give Way sign R
'Pocklington 2', then immediately L
at next T-j (same sign)

18 After 3 km (2 miles) at roundabout on the edge of Pocklington
2nd exit L 'Town Centre,
Driffield 16, Bridlington 28', then
shortly, at T-j R onto Market Street
'Town Centre' to return to the start

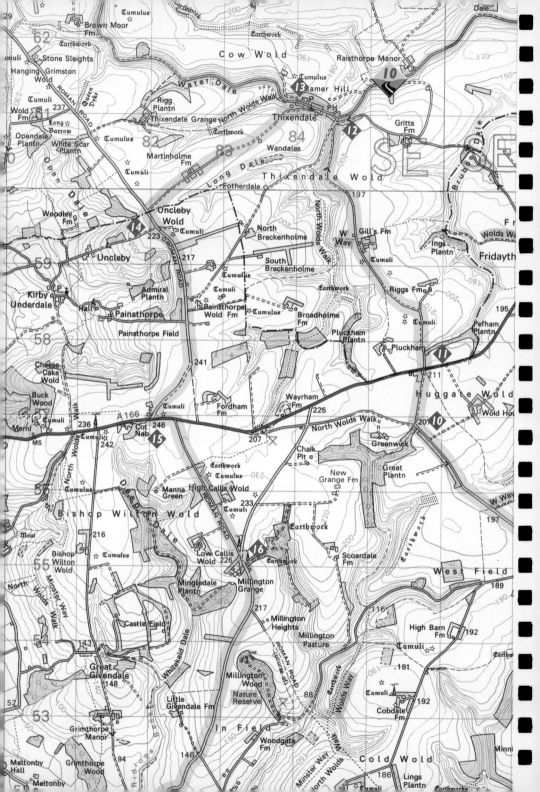

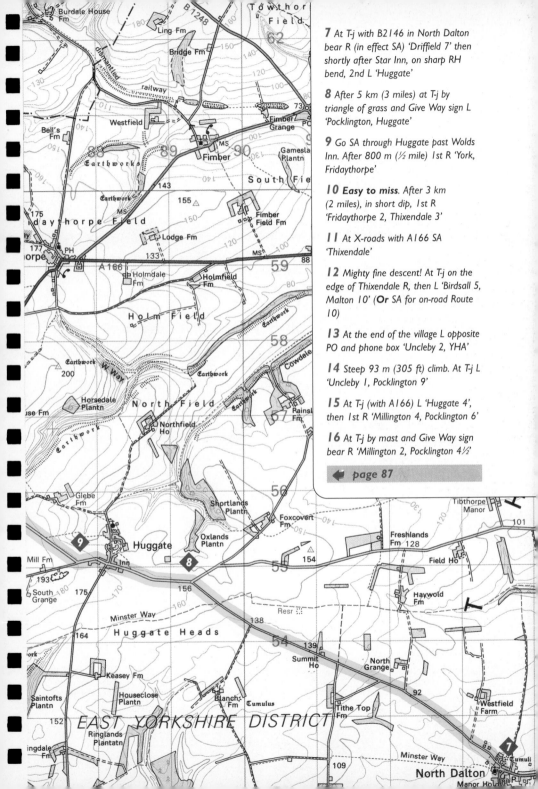

7 At T-j with B2146 in North Dalton bear R (in effect SA) 'Driffield 7' then shortly after Star Inn, on sharp RH bend, 2nd L 'Huggate'

8 After 5 km (3 miles) at T-j by triangle of grass and Give Way sign L 'Pocklington, Huggate'

9 Go SA through Huggate past Wolds Inn. After 800 m (½ mile) 1st R 'York, Fridaythorpe'

10 *Easy to miss.* After 3 km (2 miles), in short dip, 1st R 'Fridaythorpe 2, Thixendale 3'

11 At X-roads with A166 SA 'Thixendale'

12 Mighty fine descent! At T-j on the edge of Thixendale R, then L 'Birdsall 5, Malton 10' (**Or** SA for on-road Route 10)

13 At the end of the village L opposite PO and phone box 'Uncleby 2, YHA'

14 Steep 93 m (305 ft) climb. At T-j L 'Uncleby 1, Pocklington 9'

15 At T-j (with A166) L 'Huggate 4', then 1st R 'Millington 4, Pocklington 6'

16 At T-j by mast and Give Way sign bear R 'Millington 2, Pocklington 4½'

◀ page 87

13 Lanes across the Wolds, east of Market Weighton

This ride starts by skirting the edge of the Wolds between Market Weighton and Pocklington, passing the landscaped estate of Londesborough House. Northeast of Pocklington and Millington the ride follows one of the loveliest valleys in all the Wolds, climbing gradually between the steep grassy slopes up to the high point of the ride just west of Huggate. A long, gentle 153-m (500-ft) descent over the next 11 km (7 miles) drops you in Kirkburn, one of the few places along the route where refreshments are available. The ride heads south on a tiny lane between the busy parallel roads of the A164 and the B1248. The towering spire of the church at South Dalton draws you through the attractive village and estate around Dalton Hall. The final stage of the ride runs alongside the dismantled railway that used to connect Market Weighton with Beverley.

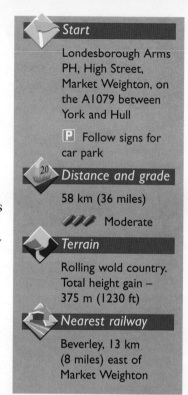

Start

Londesborough Arms PH, High Street, Market Weighton, on the A1079 between York and Hull

P Follow signs for car park

Distance and grade

58 km (36 miles)

Moderate

Terrain

Rolling wold country. Total height gain – 375 m (1230 ft)

Nearest railway

Beverley, 13 km (8 miles) east of Market Weighton

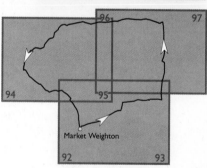

Market Weighton

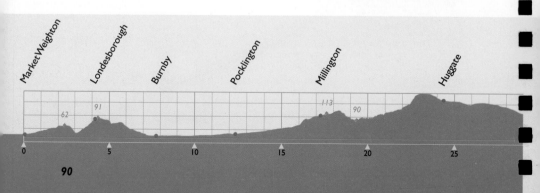

Market Weighton 1

The birthplace of the tallest Englishman recorded, William Bradley, who stood 2.36 m (7 ft 9 in). His huge chair sits in the Londesborough Arms Hotel. He died in 1825 aged 33

South Dalton 19

The church was built in the High Gothic style between 1858–61 by John Loughborough Pearson who was also the architect of Truro Cathedral. The tower is 63 m (208 ft) high 'planted like an enormous arrow in the heart of the wold'

Goodmanham *just off the route near 22*
The Norman church stands on the 7th-century pagan temple site whose high priest, Coifi, was converted to Christianity in AD 627

▲ Burnby Hall Gardens, Pocklington

Refreshments

Londesborough Arms PH 🍺, *plenty of choice in* **Market Weighton**
Feathers PH 🍺🍺, *plenty of choice in* **Pocklington**
Wolds Inn, **Huggate**
Queens Head PH 🍺, **Kirkburn**
Pipe & Glass PH 🍺, **South Dalton**

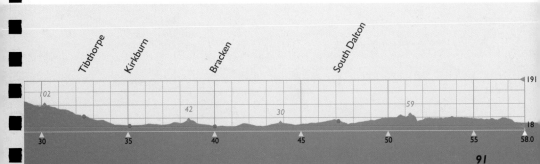

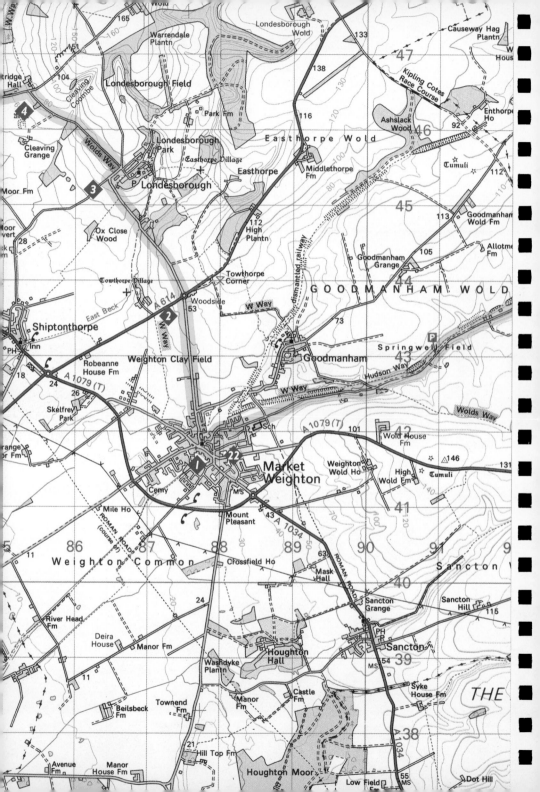

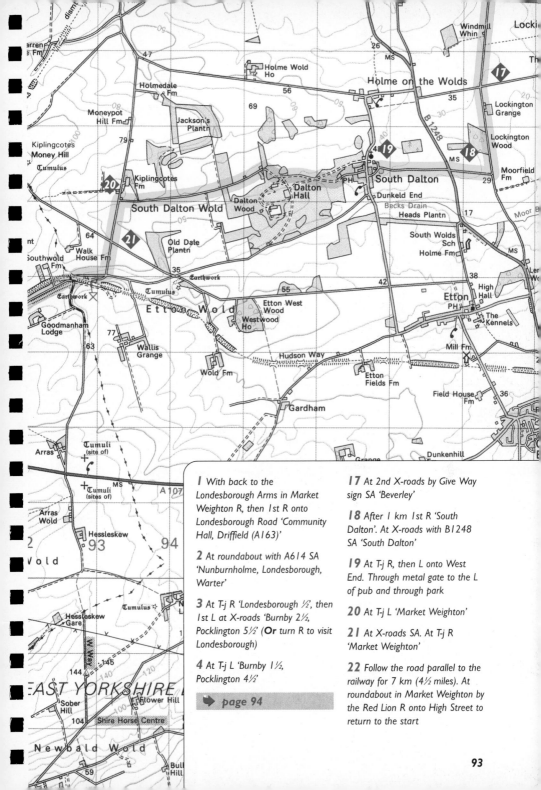

1 With back to the Londesborough Arms in Market Weighton R, then 1st R onto Londesborough Road 'Community Hall, Driffield (A163)'

2 At roundabout with A614 SA 'Nunburnholme, Londesborough, Warter'

3 At T-j R 'Londesborough ½', then 1st L at X-roads 'Burnby 2½, Pocklington 5½' (Or turn R to visit Londesborough)

4 At T-j L 'Burnby 1½, Pocklington 4½'

➡ *page 94*

17 At 2nd X-roads by Give Way sign SA 'Beverley'

18 After 1 km 1st R 'South Dalton'. At X-roads with B1248 SA 'South Dalton'

19 At T-j R, then L onto West End. Through metal gate to the L of pub and through park

20 At T-j L 'Market Weighton'

21 At X-roads SA. At T-j R 'Market Weighton'

22 Follow the road parallel to the railway for 7 km (4½ miles). At roundabout in Market Weighton by the Red Lion R onto High Street to return to the start

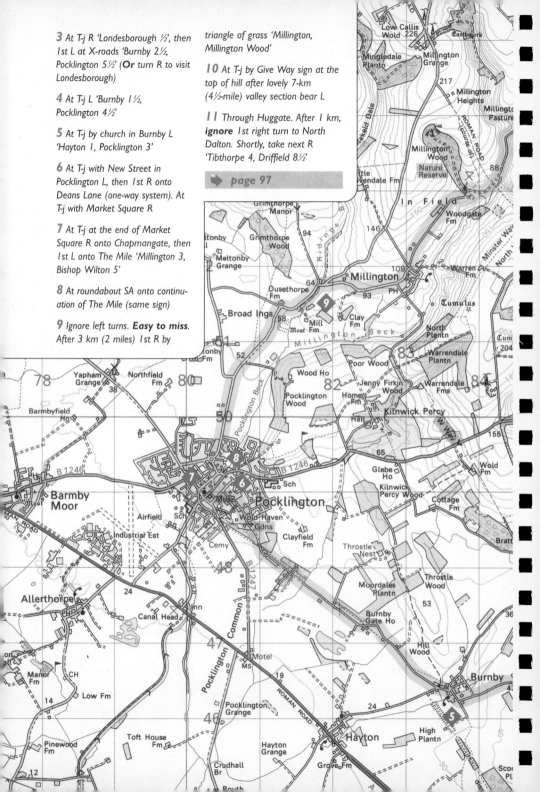

3 At T-j R 'Londesborough ½', then 1st L at X-roads 'Burnby 2½, Pocklington 5½' (**Or** turn R to visit Londesborough)

4 At T-j L 'Burnby 1½, Pocklington 4½'

5 At T-j by church in Burnby L 'Hayton 1, Pocklington 3'

6 At T-j with New Street in Pocklington L, then 1st R onto Deans Lane (one-way system). At T-j with Market Square R

7 At T-j at the end of Market Square R onto Chapmangate, then 1st L onto The Mile 'Millington 3, Bishop Wilton 5'

8 At roundabout SA onto continuation of The Mile (same sign)

9 Ignore left turns. **Easy to miss.** After 3 km (2 miles) 1st R by

triangle of grass 'Millington, Millington Wood'

10 At T-j by Give Way sign at the top of hill after lovely 7-km (4½-mile) valley section bear L

11 Through Huggate. After 1 km, **ignore** 1st right turn to North Dalton. Shortly, take next R 'Tibthorpe 4, Driffield 8½'

➤ **page 97**

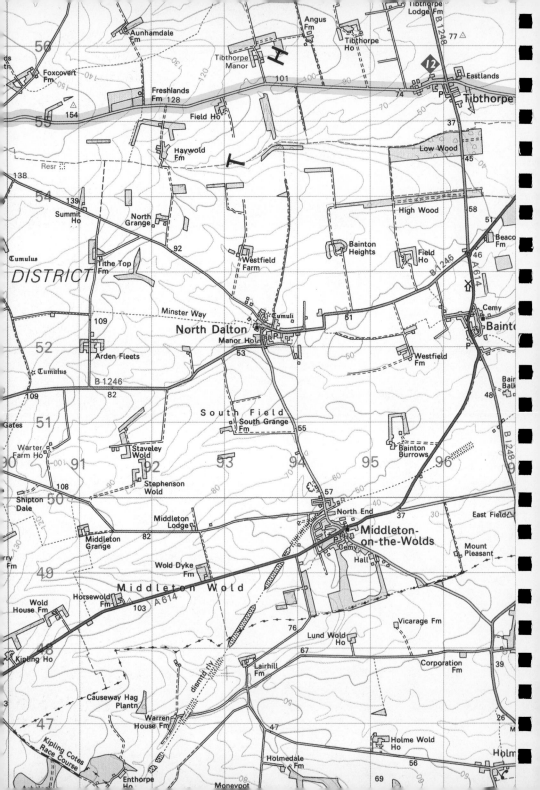

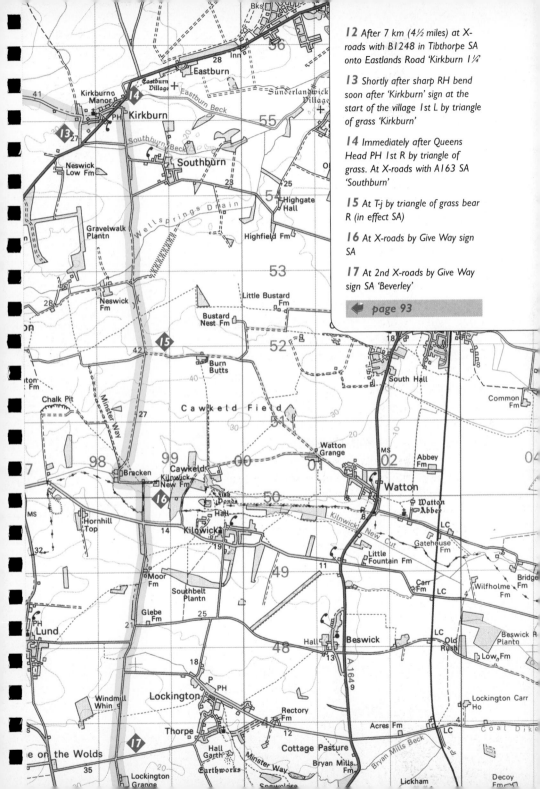

12 *After 7 km (4½ miles) at X-roads with B1248 in Tibthorpe SA onto Eastlands Road 'Kirkburn 1¼'*

13 *Shortly after sharp RH bend soon after 'Kirkburn' sign at the start of the village 1st L by triangle of grass 'Kirkburn'*

14 *Immediately after Queens Head PH 1st R by triangle of grass. At X-roads with A163 SA 'Southburn'*

15 *At T-j by triangle of grass bear R (in effect SA)*

16 *At X-roads by Give Way sign SA*

17 *At 2nd X-roads by Give Way sign SA 'Beverley'*

⬅ **page 93**

West from Beverley across the Wolds to Market Weighton

Beverley is one of the most attractive market towns in the area. The route leaves the town by way of the last surviving of the medieval gates and heads across the open rolling land between the race course and the golf course. You cross typical wold country: undulating, rich, arable land surrounded by low hedges or occasionally stone walls. North Newbald and Hotham are both attractive stone-built villages, not unlike the Cotswolds in character, both with Norman churches. The route turns north to Market Weighton, formerly the junction of several railway lines, one of which has been converted to recreational use. The church in South Dalton rises high above the surrounding wold country and is the most notable landmark on the return route from Middleton-on-the-Wolds. The ride continues south to pick up the outward route near to the golf course on the edge of Beverley.

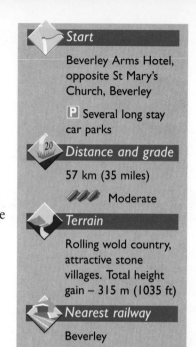

Start

Beverley Arms Hotel, opposite St Mary's Church, Beverley

P Several long stay car parks

Distance and grade

57 km (35 miles)

Moderate

Terrain

Rolling wold country, attractive stone villages. Total height gain – 315 m (1035 ft)

Nearest railway

Beverley

Refreshments

White Horse PH, plenty of choice in **Beverley**
Gnu PH, Tiger PH, **North Newbald**
Hotham Arms, **Hotham**
Londesborough Arms PH, plenty of choice in **Market Weighton**
Wellington Inn, **Lund**
Pipe & Glass PH, **South Dalton**
Light Dragoon PH, **Etton**

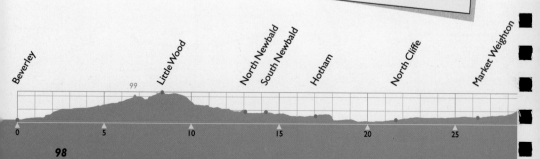

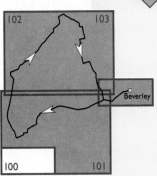

Beverley 1
Notable buildings include the 13th-century Minster, the 14th-century Church of St Mary and many Georgian houses. The North Bar (through which the route passes) is the sole survivor of five medieval gates. It was rebuilt 1409–10. The Guildhall's Heritage Centre illustrates Beverley's history. The Museum of Army Transport is crammed with military vehicles

North Newbald 4
The village has clusters of whitewashed cottages and a fine Norman church. The Northern Shire Horse Centre displays this horse breed, vintage farming implements and a farmhouse kitchen

▼ Beverley Minster

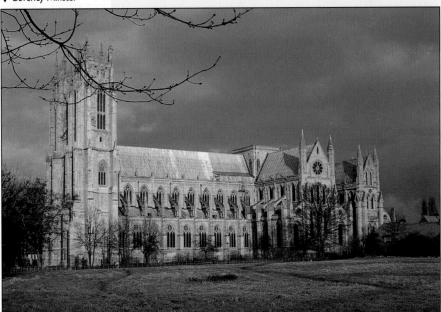

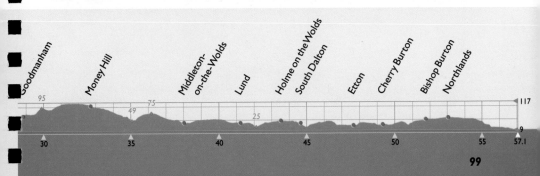

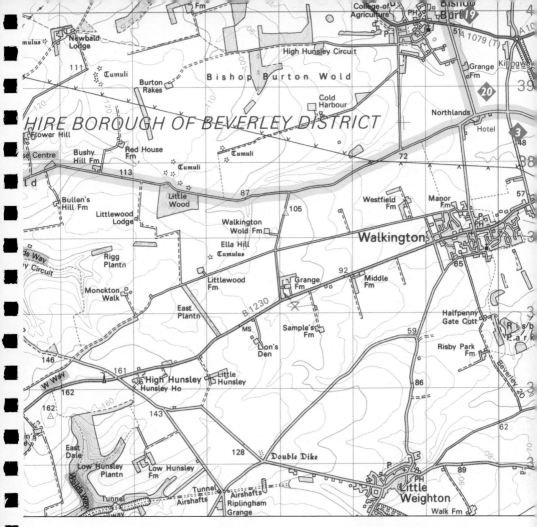

1 With back to the Beverley Arms Hotel (oposite St Mary's Church) L through the gate in the town wall, then L again by the Rose & Crown PH onto York Road 'Hull, York (A1079)'

2 After 800 m (½ mile) 1st L opposite race course '7.5 ton weight limit'

3 At X-roads after 2 km (1½ miles) SA 'North Newbald'

4 Follow this lane for 10 km (6 miles). At T-j by the village green in North Newbald L between The Gnu PH and The Tiger PH, then just past the church turn L on South Newbald Road

5 At X-roads with A1034 at the end of South Newbald Road SA 'Hotham. 7.5 ton weight limit'

6 In Hotham, opposite the Hotham Arms PH turn R past the war memorial 'North Cave 2'

7 At X-roads at the bottom of the hill R 'South Cliffe 1½, North Cliffe 2'

➭ page 102

19 At X-roads with A1079 SA 'Walkington 2'

20 At T-j with manor house ahead L 'Beverley'. (Rejoin outward route). At X-roads SA 'Beverley'

21 At T-j (with the busy A1035) after the golf course turn R. In Beverley, at traffic lights by the Rose & Crown PH turn R to return to the start

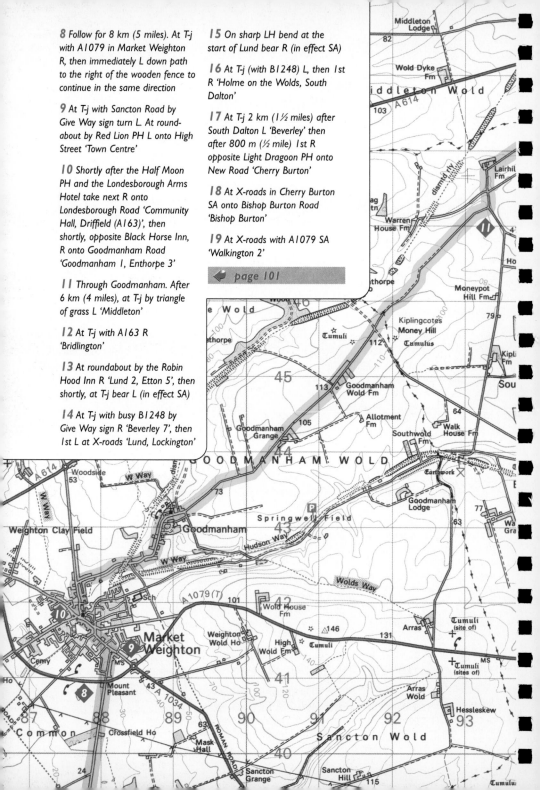

8 Follow for 8 km (5 miles). At T-j with A1079 in Market Weighton R, then immediately L down path to the right of the wooden fence to continue in the same direction

9 At T-j with Sancton Road by Give Way sign turn L. At roundabout by Red Lion PH L onto High Street 'Town Centre'

10 Shortly after the Half Moon PH and the Londesborough Arms Hotel take next R onto Londesborough Road 'Community Hall, Driffield (A163)', then shortly, opposite Black Horse Inn, R onto Goodmanham Road 'Goodmanham 1, Enthorpe 3'

11 Through Goodmanham. After 6 km (4 miles), at T-j by triangle of grass L 'Middleton'

12 At T-j with A163 R 'Bridlington'

13 At roundabout by the Robin Hood Inn R 'Lund 2, Etton 5', then shortly, at T-j bear L (in effect SA)

14 At T-j with busy B1248 by Give Way sign R 'Beverley 7', then 1st L at X-roads 'Lund, Lockington'

15 On sharp LH bend at the start of Lund bear R (in effect SA)

16 At T-j (with B1248) L, then 1st R 'Holme on the Wolds, South Dalton'

17 At T-j 2 km (1½ miles) after South Dalton L 'Beverley' then after 800 m (½ mile) 1st R opposite Light Dragoon PH onto New Road 'Cherry Burton'

18 At X-roads in Cherry Burton SA onto Bishop Burton Road 'Bishop Burton'

19 At X-roads with A1079 SA 'Walkington 2'

◀ page 101

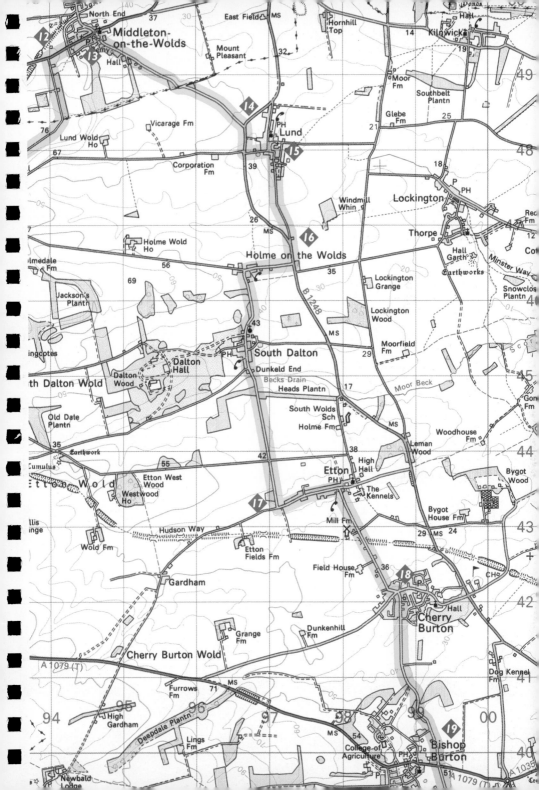

Round Hill and the moors east of Clay Bank

Start

The Clay Bank Forestry Commission car park on the B1257 between Helmsley and Middlesborough

P As above

Distance and grade

19 km (12 miles)

///// Strenuous

In their northwest corner, the North Yorkshire Moors, which are also known as the Cleveland Hills, rise to their highest point at Round Hill on Urra Moor. This means that the views are magnificent and it is well worth leaving this short but energetic ride to a fine day so that your exertions are rewarded with excellent visibility. The ride starts by meandering for 8 km (5 miles) on a broad forestry track. There are views out west across the farmland and occasional glimpses of the steep escarpment up to your right. A 213-m (700-ft) climb up a broad, stone track takes you to the top of the escarpment where the views are so good that you have plenty of excuses for stops on the way up – whether you choose to cycle or walk. The ascent continues with the Cleveland Way joining from the left. At Bloworth Crossing the ride turns west and after passing the highest point on the Yorkshire Moors you arrive at the edge of the escarpment. Be prepared, unless you have a fully suspended bike and you are technically proficient, to walk down a fair proportion of the descent.

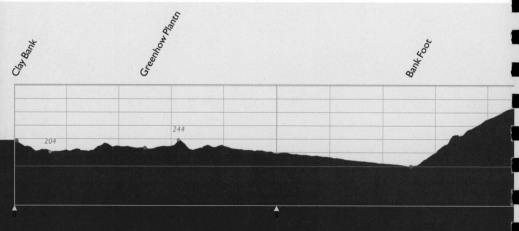

Forestry; steep hillside tracks; open moorland. Total height gain – 410 m (1345 ft)

Nearest railway

Battersby Junction, 1 km from the route at Bank Foot, instruction 3

The Cleveland Hills

This great mass of sandstone hills runs in high ridges separated by secluded valleys and patches of open moorland; one of these is Urra Moor, at 454 m (1490 ft) – the highest point in the hills. The moorlands are famous for the bilberries that grow here, possibly an important part of the diet of the lost civilisation that left their burial chambers (tumuli) scattered all over the region

Great Ayton *8 km (5 miles) north of 3* James Cook's boyhood school is now a museum. An obelisk made of rocks brought back from Point Hicks, the first part of Australia sighted on the voyage of discovery, stands on the site of his cottage

Refreshments

Dudley Arms PH 🍺*,* **Ingleby Greenhow** *(1 km off the route at instruction 3)*

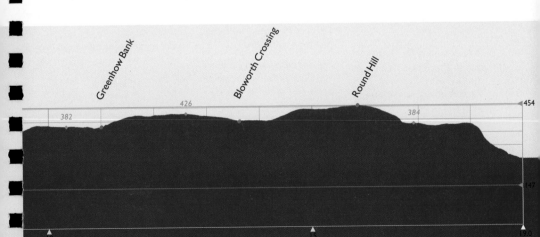

1 Exit the Forestry Commission Cleveland Forest car park at Clay Bank on the B1257 and turn L steeply downhill 'Ingleby Greenhow 2½'

2 **Easy to miss**. Do not lose control! After 800 m (½ mile) 1st R onto Forestry Commission track 'No admittance to unauthorised vehicles'

3 Follow the track for 8 km (5 miles) ignoring turnings to right and left. At T-j with tarmac by farmhouse turn R uphill

4 Through gate onto track and continue SA steeply uphill on broad

▲ Roseberry Topping from the moors

stone track, ignoring turnings to left and right. At the top, the Cleveland Way joins from the left by a green metal gate

5 A 2nd bridleway joins from the left. Climb to the standing stones at the brow of the hill, then start descending. At major X-roads of tracks with gated, dismantled railway path to the left ('Footpath only') turn R 'Cleveland Way'. (**For** link to off-road Route 7 from Kirkbymoorside, to enjoy the full length of Rudland Rigg, continue SA at X-roads and join the other ride at instructions 10/11)

6 (Main route.) After 275 m (300 yd), ignore 1st left by 'Cleveland Way' sign, 180 m (200 yd) further on take the next link track to the L

7 Climb to the brow (trig point to the right). At major fork bear R

8 Very steep, paved section where you are advised to walk. Please do not add to erosion problems and show consideration to other path users. At T-j with B1257 R for 400 m (¼ mile) to return to the start

Take care not to mistake the faded yellow line of the national park boundary for the solid yellow line of the route

2 *Beacon Hill and Great Fryup Dale, from Danby*

Start

Danby Moors Centre, near Danby and Castleton, 16 km (10 miles) southeast of Guisborough (GR 716084)

P As above

Distance and grade

28 km (17 miles)

///// Strenuous

Terrain

Moorland; river valley; farmland. Total height gain – 530 m (1740 ft)

Nearest railway

Danby

*F*rom the Moors Centre at Danby the route climbs steeply up to the first high point at Beacon Hill where there are panoramic views out to sea, up towards Tees Dale and south towards the main bulk of the moors. A dream descent over 6 km (4 miles), with a mixture of tarmac and track, drops you back down into the Esk Valley north of Glaisdale. A steep climb on tarmac takes you through Glaisdale – your last chance of refreshment on the ride. From here there is a steady climb on an excellent stone track across heather-clad Glaisdale Moor to join a minor road. The bridleway that leads off this and around the rim of the mouth-watering Great Fryup Dale is the crux of the ride. Although it is a well-defined track, this ride should not be attempted in poor visibility as the moors are fairly featureless in the mist and fog. Once around the edge of the dale and back onto the lane network you have a choice: a fast and furious tarmac descent on a quiet lane or a slower, rougher off-road route through farmland. The off-road alternative should only be attempted from late spring to late autumn as it will be hard going with boggy patches and mud at other times of the year.

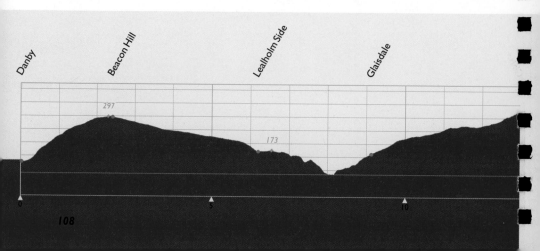

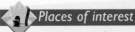

Places of interest

Danby and Danby Rigg 1

Danby's main street heads towards the heather moorlands. Red stone houses dot the landscape. The railway through Eskdale runs through the village. The arrival of the line encouraged Danby's development in the 19th century and helps to explain why the present-day village is centred almost 3 km (2 miles) northeast of its imposing church of St Hilda. Set in Danby Dale, beyond the adjoining village of Ainthorpe, the church dates from Saxon times. About 1 km southeast of Danby the remains of Danby Castle, with its dungeons intact, are incorporated in a farmhouse. The castle, built in the 14th century, was the home of Catherine Parr before she became the sixth wife of Henry VIII

Lealholm 800 m (½ mile) south of 5 Stone cottages, roofed with slates or tiles, hem the lane that leads up the dale towards Danby. One bears a carved inscription 'Loyal Order of Ancient Shepherds' with lodge insignia and the date 1873 in Roman numerals. The stonework of the Wesleyan Chapel was carved by the poet, preacher and mason John Castillo. He was a 'lantern saint', one of the early followers of John Wesley who met at night and lit their way with lanterns made from cow horns. Marks on the chapel wall show the flood height in July 1930 when the Esk burst its banks

Refreshments

Duke of Wellington PH, **Danby**
Cafe at **Danby Moors Centre**
Anglers Rest PH, **Glaisdale**

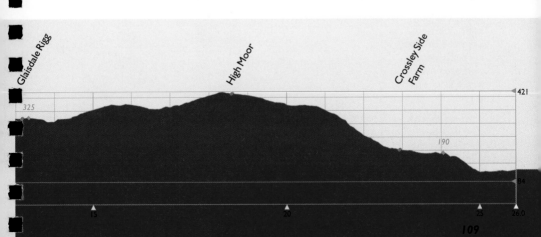

1 Exit the Danby Moors Centre car park turn R, then 1st road R 'Danby Beacon 1½'

2 Climb steeply. Immediately after the cattle grid 1st road L (NS)

3 At the beacon R 'Lealholm 3¾'

4 After 3 km (2 miles) of wonderful descent follow the main track as it swings R by wooden post with fish figure

5 At T-j with tarmac bear L (in effect SA). At T-j by small triangle of grass R 'Lealholm ½, Rosedale', then shortly 1st road to the L 'No through road, Lealholmside'. Past lovely old stone barns and fork R

6 Follow the lane as it turns to track at the farm. Cross bridge over railway, then cross the river via wooden bridge near to railway arch

7 Short steep climb. At T-j bear R (in effect SA). At X-roads in Glaisdale SA. Climb on tarmac lane past 'Unsuitable for motors' sign and continue in same direction as tarmac turns to track at gate

8 Stay on the main stone track bearing R and ignoring two tracks to the left. At fork of tracks on level section ignore track to the right

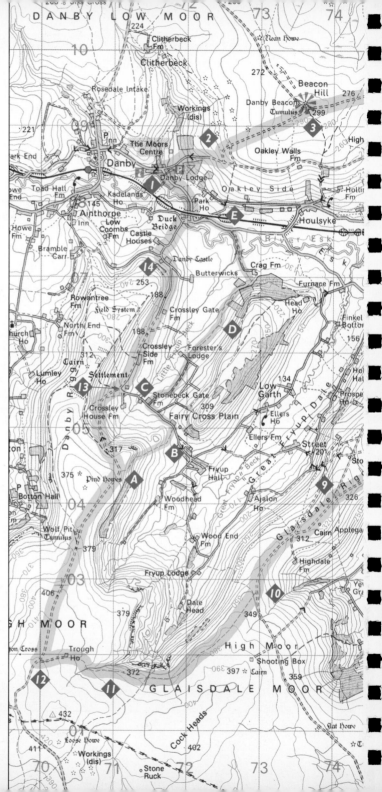

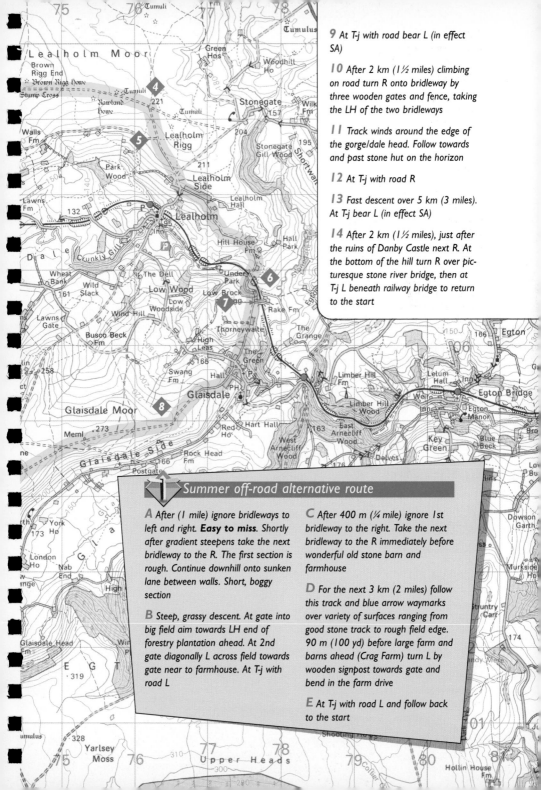

9 At T-j with road bear L (in effect SA)

10 After 2 km (1½ miles) climbing on road turn R onto bridleway by three wooden gates and fence, taking the LH of the two bridleways

11 Track winds around the edge of the gorge/dale head. Follow towards and past stone hut on the horizon

12 At T-j with road R

13 Fast descent over 5 km (3 miles). At T-j bear L (in effect SA)

14 After 2 km (1½ miles), just after the ruins of Danby Castle next R. At the bottom of the hill turn R over picturesque stone river bridge, then at T-j L beneath railway bridge to return to the start

1 Summer off-road alternative route

A After (1 mile) ignore bridleways to left and right. **Easy to miss.** Shortly after gradient steepens take the next bridleway to the R. The first section is rough. Continue downhill onto sunken lane between walls. Short, boggy section

B Steep, grassy descent. At gate into big field aim towards LH end of forestry plantation ahead. At 2nd gate diagonally L across field towards gate near to farmhouse. At T-j with road L

C After 400 m (¼ mile) ignore 1st bridleway to the right. Take the next bridleway to the R immediately before wonderful old stone barn and farmhouse

D For the next 3 km (2 miles) follow this track and blue arrow waymarks over variety of surfaces ranging from good stone track to rough field edge. 90 m (100 yd) before large farm and barns ahead (Crag Farm) turn L by wooden signpost towards gate and bend in the farm drive

E At T-j with road L and follow back to the start

3 Along the railway path between Whitby and Scarborough

The dismantled railway path between Whitby and Scarborough provides some rare, easy off-road cycling in the area covered by this book. Unusually, for a line of this length, it is all intact from the outskirts of Whitby to the outskirts of Scarborough. Another oddity of this old railway line is the climbing along the route: Ravenscar lies at over 190 m (623 ft) above sea level. Even between Whitby and Robin Hood's Bay you face a climb of 130 m (425 ft). These climbs mean that some of the views out to sea are spectacular. It is suggested that you try the Whitby–Ravenscar–Whitby section as this is the most scenic stretch; however, if you wish to go all the way to Scarborough, there is a gentle descent over 16 km (10 miles) from Ravenscar through predominantly wooded cuttings to the outskirts of the town.

NB The railway path is also popular with walkers and horse riders; please show consideration.

Start

The Tourist Information Centre in Whitby (**Or** the cemetery just south of Whitby off the A171 at GR 902098, instructions 3/4)

P Cheapest long stay parking on Church Street on the east side of River Esk (**Or** at cemetery mentioned above)

Distance and grade

Return trip from Whitby to:

Robin Hood's Bay 22 km (14 miles)

Easy

Ravenscar 35 km (22 miles)

Moderate

Scarborough 72 km (45 miles)

Strenuous

Whitby

Stainsacre

High Hawsker

125

55

0

5

Terrain

Railway path climbing to 190 m (620 ft) along the coast with fine sea views. Robin Hood's Bay – 200-m (660-ft) climb. Ravenscar – 330-m (1080-ft) climb. Scarborough – 520-m (1710-ft) climb

Nearest railway

Whitby and Scarborough

Refreshments

Plenty of choice in **Whitby** Laurel PH 🏴🏴, plenty of choice in **Robin Hood's Bay** Raven Hall Hotel, Foxcliffe Tea Room, **Ravenscar** Plenty of choice in **Scarborough**

Places of interest

High Hawsker 5
Moorland village noted for its handsome stone-built farms. Nearby a curious brick structure encloses a spring once used by the nuns of Whitby Abbey

Robin Hood's Bay 7
A fishing village on a bay of the same name, where legend says Robin Hood repelled Danish invaders. The rock-floored bay is rich in fossils. The Smuggling Experience Museum recalls the surrounding area's 18th-century smuggling days

Ravenscar 11/12
The rugged headland of Old Peak at Ravenscar is owned by the National Trust. On the summit of the 183-m (600-ft) peak is the 18th-century Raven Hall, now a hotel, situated on the site of a Roman signal point

Scarborough 13
Resort, spa and fishing town with twin bays. The town has theatres, an art gallery, and museums of natural, local and archaeological history. Hundreds of oceanic species are visible from Sea Life Centre's underwater glass tunnels

Robin Hood's Bay

Fyling Old Hall

Ravenscar

195

10

15

0

18.9

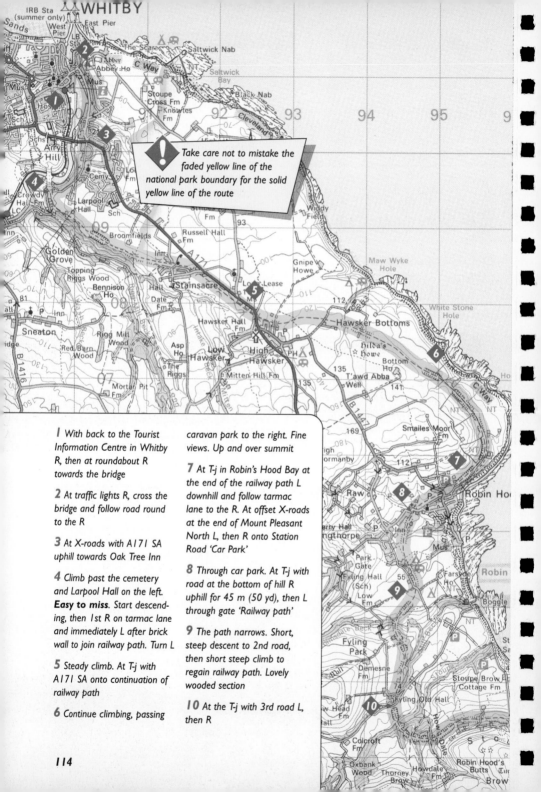

! Take care not to mistake the faded yellow line of the national park boundary for the solid yellow line of the route

1 With back to the Tourist Information Centre in Whitby R, then at roundabout R towards the bridge

2 At traffic lights R, cross the bridge and follow road round to the R

3 At X-roads with A171 SA uphill towards Oak Tree Inn

4 Climb past the cemetery and Larpool Hall on the left. **Easy to miss.** Start descending, then 1st R on tarmac lane and immediately L after brick wall to join railway path. Turn L

5 Steady climb. At T-j with A171 SA onto continuation of railway path

6 Continue climbing, passing caravan park to the right. Fine views. Up and over summit

7 At T-j in Robin's Hood Bay at the end of the railway path L downhill and follow tarmac lane to the R. At offset X-roads at the end of Mount Pleasant North L, then R onto Station Road 'Car Park'

8 Through car park. At T-j with road at the bottom of hill R uphill for 45 m (50 yd), then L through gate 'Railway path'

9 The path narrows. Short, steep descent to 2nd road, then short steep climb to regain railway path. Lovely wooded section

10 At the T-j with 3rd road L, then R

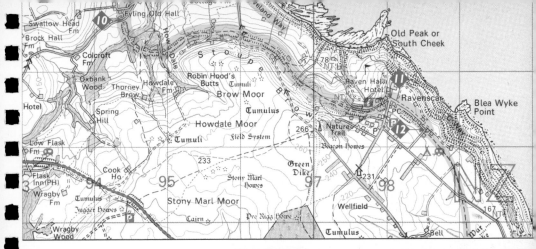

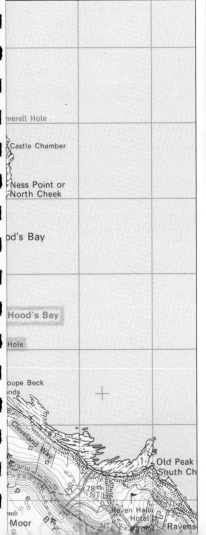

▲ Robin Hood's Bay

11 The climb ahead is now visible. At the top, at T-j by National Trust Coastal Centre L, then follow Station Road round to the right

12 It is suggested that after refreshments you turn around and return to Whitby. However, if you wish to go on to Scarborough, at the 'square' by the Foxcliffe Tearoom with 'No through road' sign ahead turn R, then L onto Loring Road. After 11 km (7 miles) at T-j with road in Cloughton SA. After Station Tea Rooms fork L. At T-j with the A165

opposite Burniston Industrial Estate L, then R soon after Hawthorn Close onto continuation of path. At the end of the path in Scalby continue on road through residential houses. At T-j at the end of Lancaster Way L, then at T-j at the end of Field Close R, then L. Follow Chichester Close round onto the restart of the railway path. Follow the path in the same direction (at one point crossing playing field/parkland) to its end by supermarket on Manor Road in Scarborough

Over Fylingdales Moor and south into Langdale Forest

Forestry tracks provide the most reliable off-road riding: the tracks are stone-based – therefore good all the year round; they are wide enough to enable cycling two or even three abreast to allow conversation; the gradients are rarely so steep that you have to get off and push and the visibility of what lies ahead tends to be fairly good so that you can really appreciate the downhills. The main drawbacks are that the views can become fairly monotonous – the attractions of coniferous trees and clearings tend to pall – and route-finding can be frustrating if newly-built tracks mean that what you see on the ground does not tally with the map. This is why a waymarked trail, with a stretch of open moorland in the middle (as you will experience on this ride), provides the best of all worlds.

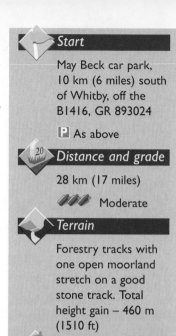

Start

May Beck car park, 10 km (6 miles) south of Whitby, off the B1416, GR 893024

P As above

Distance and grade

28 km (17 miles)

Moderate

Terrain

Forestry tracks with one open moorland stretch on a good stone track. Total height gain – 460 m (1510 ft)

Nearest railway

Whitby, 10 km (6 miles) north of the start or Scarborough, 13 km (8 miles) east of the route at Langdale End

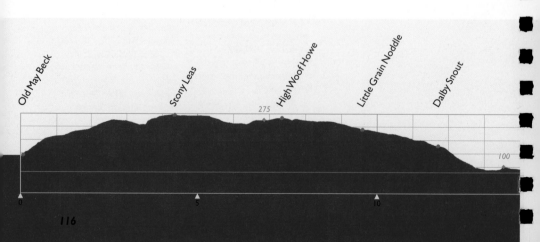

Other Forestry Commission trails

Langdale Forest *west of Scarborough*
(Parts of these are followed in the ride described). Starting point: Birch Hall Camp, GR 927925. Parking: Bickley Forest Garden Car Park. A recently planted coniferous forest covering 4500 ha (11,120 acres) which was largely formed between 1962 and 1977. The altitude rises from 100 m (330 ft) in the south to 280 m (920 ft) in the north.
Short Route, 6 km (4 miles), Purple
Medium Route, 13 km (8 miles), Green
Long Route, 24 km (15 miles), Red

Boltby Forest *8 km (5 miles) north-east of Thirsk*
Starting point: High Paradise Farm GR 503888. The forest has 500 ha (1235 acres) of mainly conifer woodland with wonderful views over the northern Vale of York. The trails are shut on pheasant shooting days (these days are displayed at High Paradise Farm).
Short Route, 6.5 km (4 miles), Green
Medium Route, 11 km (7 miles), Red
Long Route, 19 km (12 miles), Blue

Guisborough Forest *southeast of Middlesbrough*
Starting point: the car park at Pinchinthorpe Station on the Guisborough Walkway GR 584153 (west of Guisborough, on the A173 near the junction with the A171).
One route, 8 km (5 miles)
There are also large holdings in Cropton Forest, Dalby Forest and Wykeham Forest where it would be possible to devise your own routes

Refreshments

Moorcock Inn 🍴,
Langdale End

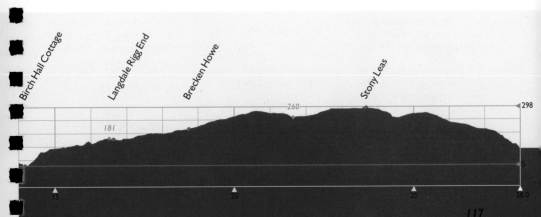

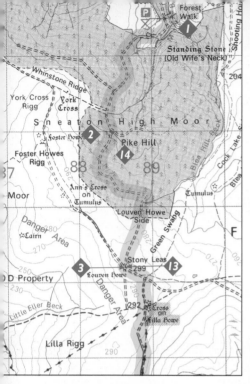
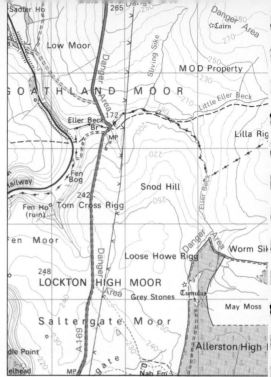

1 From the May Beck car park 10 km (6 miles) south of Whitby (GR 893024) go SA uphill on forestry track 'No unauthorised vehicles'

2 Climb steeply, enter the forest. The gradient lessens. **Ignore** 1st right by signpost. Continue uphill. Short descent, then continue climbing. At fork bear R on uphill track (black and white post)

3 Exit forest. Summit is reached with views of MOD listening station away to the right. **Ignore** left to Robin Hood's Bay (blue arrow)

4 Follow track with the perimeter fence on your right. Shortly after the start of the forestry to the left 1st L by wooden barrier. **Easy to miss.** Ignore two left turns on steady ascent. 400 m (¼ mile) after the brow of the hill take the 1st major stone track to the R

(opposite black and white post, GR 894964). Remember this point for return leg

5 After 800 m (½ mile) follow the main track round to the L, ignoring less major track to the right (GR 888961)

6 Superb 5-km (3-mile) descent. At T-j (GR 915927) turn L downhill 'Red Bike Route, North Riding Forest Park, Langdale Forest mountain bike trails'

7 Descend, then climb. At T-j (GR 923927) turn R 'Red Bike/Green Bike Routes'. Forestry road joins from the left 'Langdale mountain bike trail start'

8 Shortly, at the start of tarmac, 1st L through metal barrier 'Red Bike/Green Bike Routes', then fork R 'Red Bike/Green/Purple Bike Routes'. After 180 m (200 yd) 1st

R on steep, rutted track 'Red Bike/Green Bike Routes' (you will need to push). (**Or** for visit to Moorcock Inn at Langdale End, at the start of tarmac bear R downhill. Continue in this direction for 3 km (1¼ miles). On the return, keep bearing R and rejoin at instructions 9/10)

9 At T-j with broad forestry track bear L to continue climbing (GR 930930)

10 Ignore right and left turns for 2 km (1½ miles). At major fork of tracks with a green, metal barrier to the left and a wooden gate alongside the RH fork bear L 'Red Bike/Green Bike Routes'

11 **Ignore** four right turns (each with bike signs). At the next left turn 'Red Bike/Green Bike Routes' bear R and rejoin the outward route

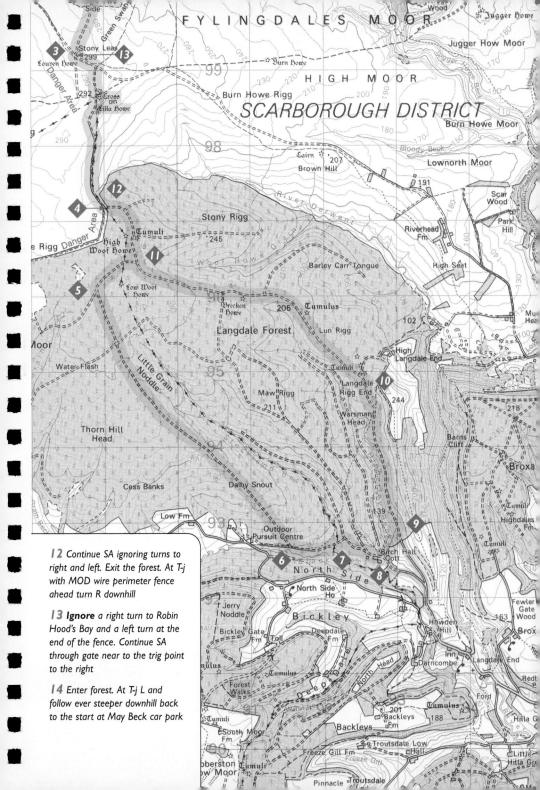

12 *Continue SA ignoring turns to right and left. Exit the forest. At T-j with MOD wire perimeter fence ahead turn R downhill*

13 Ignore *a right turn to Robin Hood's Bay and a left turn at the end of the fence. Continue SA through gate near to the trig point to the right*

14 *Enter forest. At T-j L and follow ever steeper downhill back to the start at May Beck car park*

5 Along the Cleveland Way from Sutton Bank

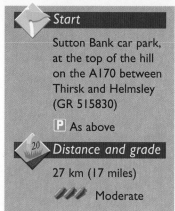

Start

Sutton Bank car park, at the top of the hill on the A170 between Thirsk and Helmsley (GR 515830)

P As above

Distance and grade

27 km (17 miles)

Moderate

Sutton Bank is one of the most dramatic and well-known features of the region. The bridleway (Cleveland Way) running north along the top of the escarpment has magnificent views out to the west. Once onto the old Hambleton Drove Road the ride bears away from the edge and across moorland on a fine stone track. This is a ride with many possible diversions and variations: the first is to follow the Cleveland Way down into Osmotherley and add on an extra northern loop to the ride; the described route turns east at the crossroads with the wonderful, old unclassified road that runs from Kepwick to Hawnby. The descent is so good and the lure of the pub in Hawnby (the only chance of refreshment near the route) may be so great that you will divert from the highlighted route and rejoin it later. After a section across open pasture you are soon faced with a steep, at times technical, descent down through woodland to the ruins of Daleside in the upper Rye Valley. A climb on tarmac follows before the last steep descent into and climb out of the valley that cuts through Yowlass Wood. Lanes are then followed back to the start.

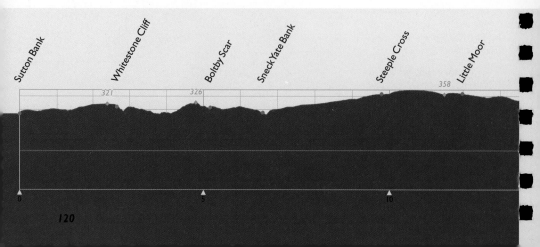

Terrain

Escarpment edge;
heather-clad moorland;
woodland and pasture.
Total height gain –
320 m (1060 ft)

Nearest railway

Thirsk, 10 km (6 miles)
west of the start

Places of interest

Sutton Bank 1

Gliders swirl above the escarpment that
rises 183 m (600 ft) from the Vale of York.
A walk leads to the White Horse of
Kilburn, created in 1857 by a local school-
master and his pupils who cut away turf to
form a white horse 96 m (314 ft) long.
Nearby, footpaths lead to the limestone
crags of Roulston Scar and the prehistoric
Caston Dikes

Hambleton Drove Road 6

An ancient cattle-driving route still in use
today, partly as a modern road and partly
as a green road

Old Byland off the route near 16

A curiosity in the village is the medieval
sundial in the church wall – it is unusable
as it was installed upside-down

Refreshments

Cafe at **Sutton Bank car park**
Hawnby PH 🍺, **Hawnby** (just off
the route at instruction 9)

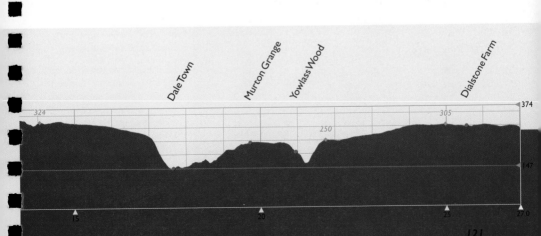

121

1 Exit Sutton Bank car park and take the road towards Cold Kirby, Old Byland and Hawnby

2 1st road L by the mast 'Boltby 3, Hawnby 5', then immediately L again by Dialstone Farm 'Bridleway'

3 Follow in the same direction along the field edge towards a clump of trees, ignoring right turns. At the trees turn R, then soon join better track contouring above the valley with fabulous views

4 Stay on the upper track above the edge of woodland following Cleveland Way signs

5 Shortly after grassy descent at gate in stone wall by signpost with 'Sutton Bank 3' bear R uphill, then R at the road

6 At X-roads at the top of the climb L 'Boltby Cycle Trails Parking, No vehicles except access'

7 As the main track swings left by a sign for cycle trails bear R (in effect SA) onto grass and stone track

8 Better quality track along the forest edge. Continue in the same direction, alongside a wall to the left. Go past a gate on the left with blue arrow and 'Beware adders' sign. At X-roads of tracks with tarmac lane to the left signposted 'Kepwick' turn R uphill 'Hawnby'

9 Fine descent. After 2 km (1½ miles), as the downhill gradient steepens alongside woodland on the left take the 1st broad stone track on the R steeply uphill. (Or for route avoiding

technical descent continue SA down into Hawnby)

10 The track surface is a mixture of stone and firm grass. At the fork of grassy tracks bear R to the right of conifer plantations

11 At X-roads of tracks in the corner of the field bounded by stone walls turn L through gate onto broad grassy track. (Or to avoid steep descent go SA, then at T-j with road R and rejoin at 17). Follow the track in the same direction towards and past stone and red-tile hay barn. The track swings R, then L to a gate in the stone wall

12 Continue SA down very steep bumpy track towards small stone cottage in the valley. At X-roads with broad, level track continue SA downhill towards house, then follow the 'Dale Town' sign (blue arrow)

13 Follow blue arrows as the track climbs gently round to the buildings of Dale Town. Through the farmyard and bear L by cattle grid onto broad stone track

14 At T-j with road turn sharp R steeply uphill. Climb steeply, then more gently. After 1 km 1st L 'Murton Grange'

15 After 1 km as the road swings left bear R (in effect SA) onto track. A track joins from the left. Shortly, leave the main track and fork L downhill on narrow grassy track 'Cold Kirby' (blue arrow)

16 Briefly rejoin main track, then turn L steeply downhill 'Bridleway' ('Private' signs indicate where you cannot go). Descend to cross stream, then a 10-minute push. At T-j with the road R

17 At T-j L towards mast. At T-j just past mast R 'Sutton Bank 1, Thirsk 6'

▲ The moors near Hawnby

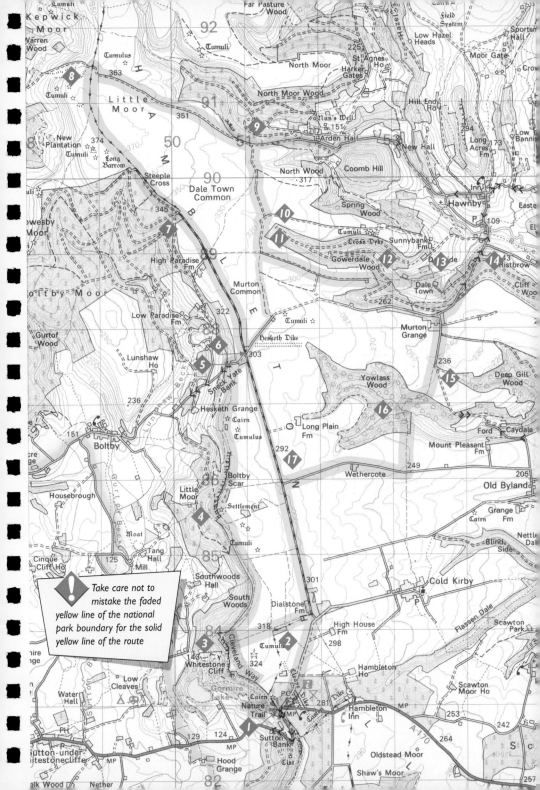

Take care not to mistake the faded yellow line of the national park boundary for the solid yellow line of the route

Cowhouse Bank, Rye Dale and Rievaulx Abbey, north of Helmsley

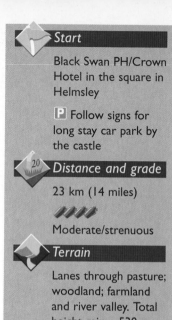

Start

Black Swan PH/Crown Hotel in the square in Helmsley

P Follow signs for long stay car park by the castle

Distance and grade

23 km (14 miles)

Moderate/strenuous

Terrain

Lanes through pasture; woodland; farmland and river valley. Total height gain – 530 m (1740 ft)

Nearest railway

Thirsk or Malton, both 20 km (12 miles) from Helmsley

Helmsley is one of the tourist centres of the North Yorkshire Moors; with its castle, wide square surrounded by attractive old buildings and fine selection of eating and drinking establishments it makes a good base for exploring the area. The ride leaves Helmsley on the minor lane that starts at the back of the square and climbs steadily over the next 10 km (6 miles), gaining over 259 m (850 ft), at first on tarmac then on a forestry track above Cowhouse Bank from where there are superb views north to the high moors. A fine, fast descent through the next section of forestry drops you onto the B1257 then down still further into the valley of the River Rye. Bridleways, byways and gently neglected lanes lead south through orchards, farms and fields, crossing a handsome stone bridge over the River Rye near to Rievaulx Abbey before the final, steep on-road climb back up to the B1257 and the long descent back to the start.

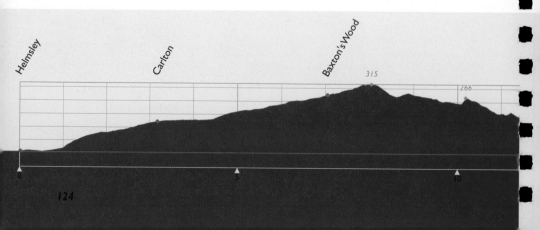

Rievaulx Abbey 11

The majestic, roofless shell of Rievaulx Abbey is striking testimony to the enterprise and skills of the Cistercian monks who founded it eight centuries ago. They came from France in 1131, to land granted to them by Walter Espec, Lord of Helmsley. The abbey was an enormous task for the brotherhood's stonemasons. To avoid rapids on the River Rye they even built a short canal along which they ferried stone from a nearby quarry. Completed in the 12th century, the abbey at one time had about 140 monks, 600 lay brothers and 12,000 sheep. The monks were also pioneers in iron-making technology. Locally-mined iron ore was smelted in four furnaces and there was a forge on the site of the present mill. Even after the Dissolution of the Monasteries in 1539, iron-making continued in Rye Dale and the first blast furnace was built there in 1576

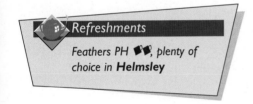

Refreshments

Feathers PH 🍴🍺, plenty of choice in **Helmsley**

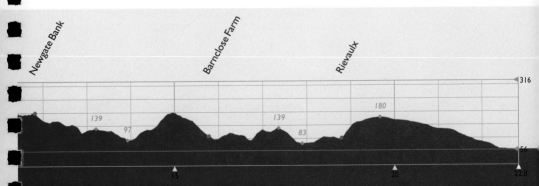

1 From the mini roundabout in the square in Helmsley take the narrow lane between the Black Swan and the Crown Hotel. Shortly, at X-roads R, then at T-j at the end of Carlton Lane L (NS)

2 Climb steadily for 5 km (3½ miles), passing through Carlton. **Easy to miss**. Go past section of forestry and track to Carlton Park Farm (both to the right). Where the woodland restarts on the right turn L onto stone track 'Newgate Bank', then fork L at Forestry Commission sign 'Cow House Bank Viewpoint'

3 Steady climb. At T-j with road R downhill. At junction of tracks at the end of tarmac turn L onto broad stone forestry track 'Footpath'

4 Fine descent. At T-j (with B1257) sharp R downhill. **Easy to miss**. Keep your brakes on! After

180 m (200 yd), just before the end of the woodland on the left turn, sharp L onto semi-hidden track 'Bridleway' (If you come to a house on your right you have gone too far)

5 Just before farm buildings R downhill towards stone farmhouse. At T-j with tarmac L 'Bridleway. Shaken Bridge'

6 At T-j with the road R downhill, cross bridge, then 1st L over cattle grid 'Shaken Bridge Farm' (blue arrow). As the concrete track swings sharp R uphill towards farm turn L through gate, then R uphill. Rejoin main stone track near to cattle grid and turn L

7 At fork of tracks bear L on lower track. As the main track swings sharp R steeply uphill bear L on less steep track. The track

climbs, then bears L downhill towards bridlegate in the corner of the field 'Barnclose Farm follow field edge'

8 Through Barnclose Farm bearing R onto tarmac lane. Follow this lane past Tylas Farm

9 **Easy to miss**. As the gradient steepens, just over 1 km after Tylas Farm, 1st L downhill on track

10 Descend, then climb. At T-j R

11 At T-j by church L steeply uphill (**Or** R to visit Rievaulx Abbey)

12 Tough climb. At T-j with B1257 R 'Helmsley 2'

13 Fine descent. In Helmsley 1st L after the church 'A170 Scarborough' to return to the start

▼ Rievaulx Terrace

Take care not to mistake the faded yellow line of the national park boundary for the solid yellow line of the route

7 Pockley Moor, Bransdale and Rudland Rigg, north of Kirkbymoorside

Start

The White Horse PH in Kirkbymoorside, on the A170 between Helmsley and Pickering

P Plenty of parking in the broad main street of Kirkbymoorside

Distance and grade

36 km (22 miles)

Strenuous

Although this is a relatively long off-road ride, more than half is on quiet or dead-end lanes and the vast majority of the climbing is on good surfaces. The first off-road section comes 8 km (5 miles) from the start, linking Kirk Dale with Beadlam Rigg. The tarmac lane is followed to its end at High Farm and soon a sunken, stony and sandy track is joined that continues to climb north onto Hagg Common and Pockley Moor. Suddenly a panorama opens up ahead. The track joins the loop road that goes north around Bransdale before climbing up onto Rudland Rigg – a fine, broad, stone track over the roof of the moors and one of the best off-road delights in the National Park.

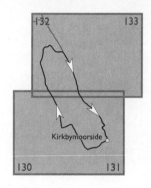

At this point you can easily link with off-road Route 1 by turning north along Rudland Rigg. The route described heads south, continuing to climb then starting the heavenly descent towards Gillamoor, from where tracks and bridleways are followed right into the heart of Kirkbymoorside.

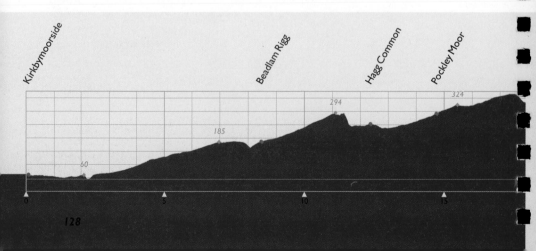

Arable fields; pasture
and high moorland.
Tracks vary in quality
from excellent to
trashed by four-wheel-
drive vehicles.
Total height gain –
580 m (1900 ft)

Nearest railway

Malton, 18 km
(11 miles) southeast of
the start

Places of interest

Kirkdale 4

The wooded valley of Kirk Dale ('valley of
the church') takes its name from the little
St Gregory's Minster, a late Saxon Church
with many details unaltered. In the porch
is a Saxon sundial with an inscription
which, roughly translated, reads: 'Orm,
Gamel's son, bought St Gregory's Minster
when it was all ruined and fallen down,
and he caused it to be built new from the
ground in the days of Edward and in the
days of Tosti the Earl. This is the day's sun
marker at each hour. Haworth made me
and Brand, priests'. Kirkdale Cave, discovered in 1821, contained the bones of many
Ice Age animals.

Farndale east of 10-12

The valley is carpeted with daffodils in
spring; the local inhabitants claim that this
inspired Wordsworth

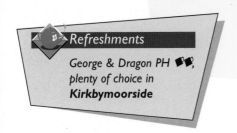

Refreshments

George & Dragon PH,
plenty of choice in
Kirkbymoorside

Cockayne

369   372

Rudland Rigg

Gillamoor

375

244

180

150

80

36

20   25   30   35 35.8

1 With back to the White Horse PH in Kirkbymoorside L along West End. Just before T-j with A170 R into layby, then follow path parallel to main road

2 At T-j with minor lane R. At X-roads SA 'Kildale ¼, Helmsley 4¾'

3 Through ford. Ignore 1st right to St Gregory Minster. After 800 m (½ mile) take next R 'Skiplam only'

4 **Easy to miss.** Follow for 5 km (3 miles) climbing steadily and passing a row of brick cottages on your left. 800 m (½ mile) after passing a left turn to Ewe Coat Farm on your left next road L 'Link'

5 At T-j (white gates and 'Private Road' sign to the right) go SA onto bridleway (the 1st 45 m (50 yd) may be overgrown). Descend, at X-roads with wider track SA, then up and along field edge. At T-j with road R

6 Tarmac turns to track at High Farm. Through strip of woodland and onto broad sandstone track between heather climbing to summit

7 Follow this track in the same direction for 5 km (3½ miles), descending then climbing. Continue SA at each X-roads of tracks. **Take care** - parts of the track have been badly eroded

➡ **page 133**

12 'Roof of the world' descent. At T-j with road L 'Fadmoor 2½, Kirkbymoorside 4½'

13 Descend, then climb. Take the 1st road L by triangle of grass 'Gillamoor'

14 At T-j in Gillamoor L, then R 'Kirkbymoorside 2'. Shortly, as the road swings right, bear L (in effect SA) onto narrow tarmac lane

15 Tarmac turns to track. At T-j R 'High Park' (blue arrow). At the farm bear L away from tarmac, through gate and onto stone track alongside field

16 The track swings L and passes golf course. At fork bear L on upper track

17 At T-j shortly after the start of houses R, then at next T-j (with Park Lane/Castlegate Lane) R again. At the roundabout bear L downhill to return to the start

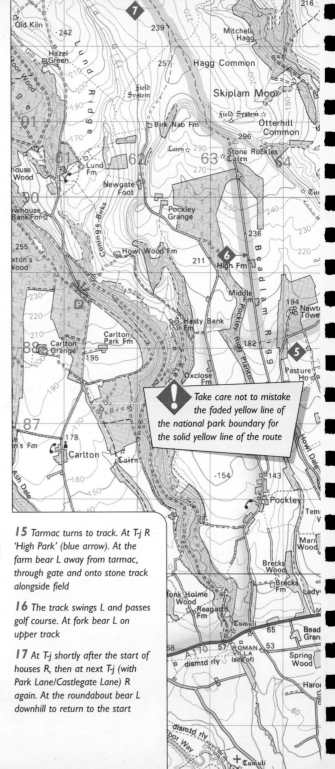

! Take care not to mistake the faded yellow line of the national park boundary for the solid yellow line of the route

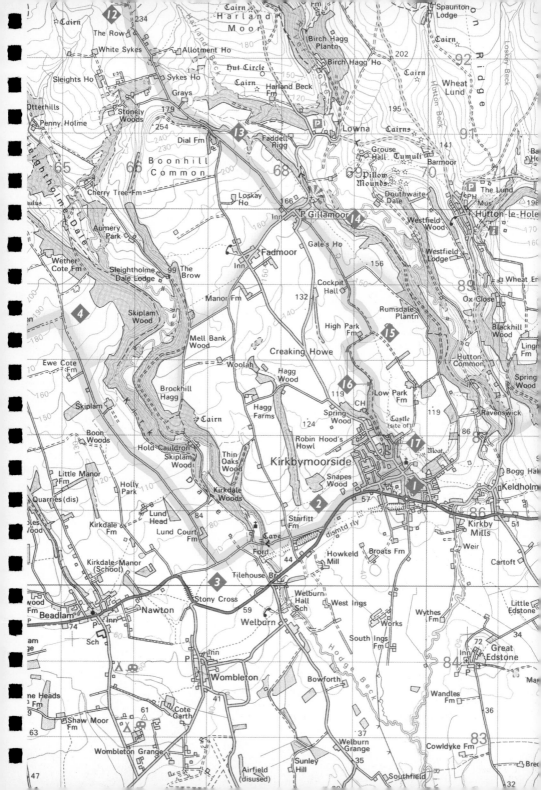

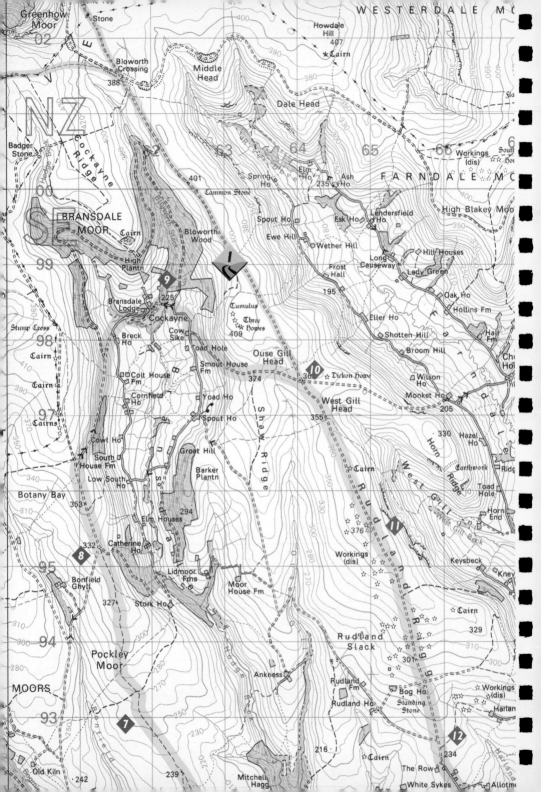

▲ *Farndale*

7 *Follow this track in the same direction for 5 km (3½ miles), descending then climbing. Continue SA at each X-roads of tracks.* **Take care** *- parts of the track have been badly eroded*

8 *At T-j with road bear R*

9 *Follow gated road up, then steeply down. At T-j R 'Kirkbymoorside'. After climbing steeply for 800 m (½ mile), opposite the 1st farm on the right turn L alongside stone wall*

10 *Climb steeply. At major X-roads of tracks R (**Or** L for off-road Route 1)*

11 *Continue climbing for further 2 km (1½ miles) to trig point*

12 *'Roof of the world' descent. At T-j with road L 'Fadmoor 2½, Kirkbymoorside 4½'*

◀ page 130

Rosedale Abbey, north from Hutton-le-Hole

8

Start

The Ryedale Museum, Hutton-le-Hole, north of the A170 near to Kirkbymoorside

P Follow the sign-posted car park

Distance and grade

22 km (13 miles)

Moderate (one steep on-road push)

Terrain

Pasture and farmland, heather and fern-covered low moorland. Total height gain – 380 m (1250 ft)

Nearest railway

Malton, 24 km (14 miles) south of the start

One of the few roads that goes right over the top of the moors passes through Hutton-le-Hole, climbs to almost 426 m (1400 ft) over Blakey Ridge before dropping down to Castleton. It is not until after Rosedale Abbey that this ride eventually climbs high onto the moors; it starts by heading away from them to the south on a sunken lane through woodland then across arable fields to Appleton-le-Moors. The road drops down into the valley of the River Seven which is followed north for 8 km (5 miles) on a low, moorland track that will involve some pushing on the rockier sections. It is, nevertheless, a delightful section particularly from late spring to late autumn when the ground is firm enough to be rideable. The climb up Rosedale Chimney is one of the steepest roads in the country. Your exertions are rewarded with ever-wider views and after the top a long descent that, with the exception of one short climb after Loskey Beck, is an unbroken descent for 7 km (4 miles) back down to Hutton-le-Hole.

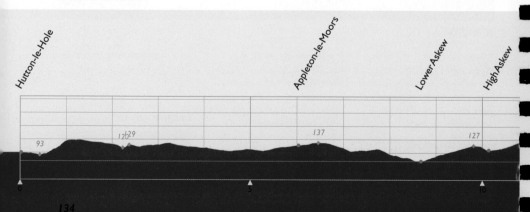

Hutton-le-Hole 1

Neat cottages and houses of pale stone, many roofed with weathered red tiles, are scattered along both sides of a grassy ravine carved by Hutton Beck as it rushes south from the moors. 'Hoton' was listed in the Domesday Book of 1086, but did not really develop until the 17th century, when it became a refuge for persecuted Quakers. The Ryedale Folk Museum holds reconstructed buildings ranging from an Elizabethan glass furnace to medieval long-house examples

Rosedale Abbey 10

Despite its name, the village does not have an abbey. Close to the little Victorian church are a few fragments of a stone buttress – all that remains of a Cistercian nunnery established in the mid-12th century. Iron was the *raison d'etre* of the village. In the 13th century, rich iron finds in the surrounding hills attracted the attention of the monks of Byland Abbey, near Helmsley. Interest in local iron was revived in the 19th century and a furnace was built on the hill above Rosedale; its chimney, the Rosedale Chimney, was a prominent landmark until 1972

Refreshments

Crown PH 🍺, tea rooms, **Hutton-le-Hole**
Appleton Hall Hotel, Moors Inn, **Appleton-le-Moors**
White Horse Farm Hotel, on the route above **Rosedale Abbey**
Milburn Arms PH 🍺🍺, tea rooms, **Rosedale Abbey** (just off the route)

Rosedale Abbey

Spindle Thorn

141
126
171
311
70
15
20
21.6

1 With back to the Ryedale Museum in Hutton-le-Hole L downhill towards Kirkbymoorside. At the end of the village, immediately after crossing a stream 1st L, then bear L onto track 'Link, Cropton 5'

2 The steep, sunken track becomes a broad track across field. Go round a RH bend, then with double wooden gates ahead (and the farm 275 m (300 yd) away) turn L onto grassier track (blue arrow)

3 Exit wood via gate into field and turn L alongside line of trees. Through 2nd gate and onto better defined track

4 At X-roads of tracks by triangle of grass R 'Bridleway, Link'

5 Broad, stone track across field. Exit via gate and continue SA (Footpath to Appleton-le-Moors is signposted to the left). At T-j with road L

6 Through Appleton-le-Moors. At the far end of the village (beyond the hotel on the left) 1st road R 'Cropton 2, Rosedale 6½'

7 Long descent. At T-j by long stone barn bear L (in effect SA) 'Lastingham 1, Hutton le Hole 2¾' then shortly, on sharp LH bend, bear R (in effect SA) onto tarmac and grass lane

8 At the gate 90 m (100 yd) before High Askew Farm turn L alongside fence then wall. The first section is among trees and will involve a mixture of cycling and pushing

9 Follow this bridleway in the same direction for 5 km (3 miles). This continues as a mixture of riding and pushing. Join a better track near to the farm and follow to the road

10 At T-j by White Horse Farm Hotel turn L uphill. (**Or** turn R downhill to visit Rosedale Abbey)

11 One of the steepest on-road climbs in the country! Long descent, then short climb beyond the brook. At T-j at the bottom of the hill R, then at T-j in Hutton-le-Hole L to return to the start

▼ Rosedale Head

9 Into the Howardian Hills, south of Hovingham

This ride from Hovingham lies between the Moors and the Wolds on the Howardian Hills. Although this is the longest off-road route in the book it can easily be shortened. As it is a low level ride and is unlikely to be affected either by moorland mists or the severe weather experienced on the high moors but it will suffer from muddy conditions through the winter and into spring. The ride starts from Hovingham – an attractive village with two good pubs and a tea shop. The houses are built of the same stone (oolitic limestone) that is found in the Cotswolds and there are many attractive stone barns and farmhouses along the way, not to mention Castle Howard – one of the country's grandest houses. The ride links lanes and tracks, some narrow and at times a little overgrown, heading generally west, south then east before coming to the best section of the whole ride – the northern edge of the 'escarpment', alongside the woodland and earthworks, with views north to the Moors.

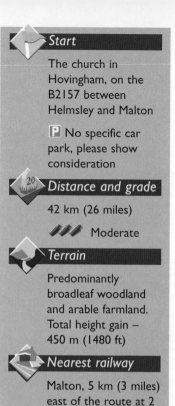

Start

The church in Hovingham, on the B2157 between Helmsley and Malton

[P] No specific car park, please show consideration

Distance and grade

42 km (26 miles)

Moderate

Terrain

Predominantly broadleaf woodland and arable farmland. Total height gain – 450 m (1480 ft)

Nearest railway

Malton, 5 km (3 miles) east of the route at 2

Refreshments

Worsley Arms Hotel 🍺, Malt Shovel PH 🍺, tea rooms, **Hovingham**
Bayhorse PH 🍺, **Terrington**
Crown & Cushion PH 🍺, **Welburn**

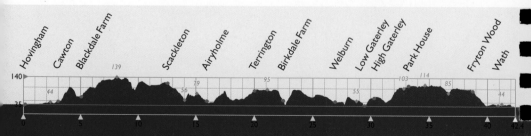

15 Long climb. At T-j with road R. At next T-j L 'Welburn 1, York 14½'

16 At X-roads by Give Way sign SA 'Welburn ½, Malton 6'. Past the Crown & Cushion PH in Welburn, then 1st road L 'Water Lane. No through road'

17 With houses ahead bear L 'Bridleway'. At X-roads of tracks SA towards wood. Through wood on well-defined track

18 At X-roads with Centenary Way near the edge of woodland SA to exit wood . At T-j with tarmac R

19 Past modern houses on left. Ignore 'Centenary Way' to the left. Go round sharp LH bend, then next R downhill towards stone barn

20 Fine gravel track ends at farmhouse. Continue SA onto rougher broad, stone track (blue arrow), then after 180 m (200 yd) turn L (blue arrow) onto broad track along field edge

21 Continue in same direction along edge of wood and past buildings of Easthorpe Stud (this is to your left). Climb through woodland. At T-j with road by triangle of grass L

22 Immediately after brow of hill 1st track R 'Park House, Bridleway'. After 90 m (100 yd) L onto yard, then L through double gates to follow track around the outside of the property (i.e. leave buildings to your right)

23 Through bridlegate and along edge of woodland. Over the next 4 km (2½ miles) follow track downhill ignoring Centenary Way to the left. Exit woodland and continue in same direction along top edge of field. At X-roads with road SA onto track (blue arrow)

➧ page 141

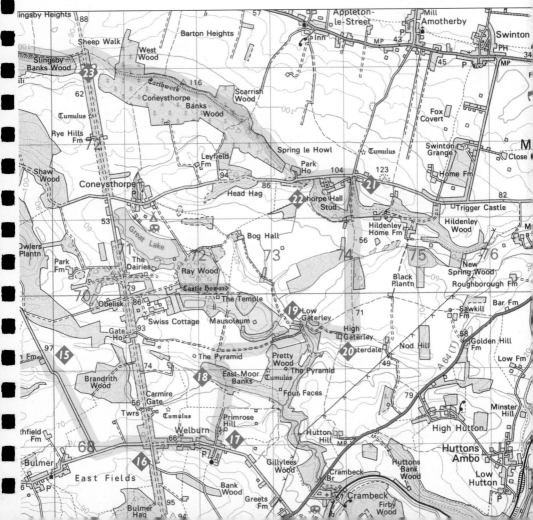

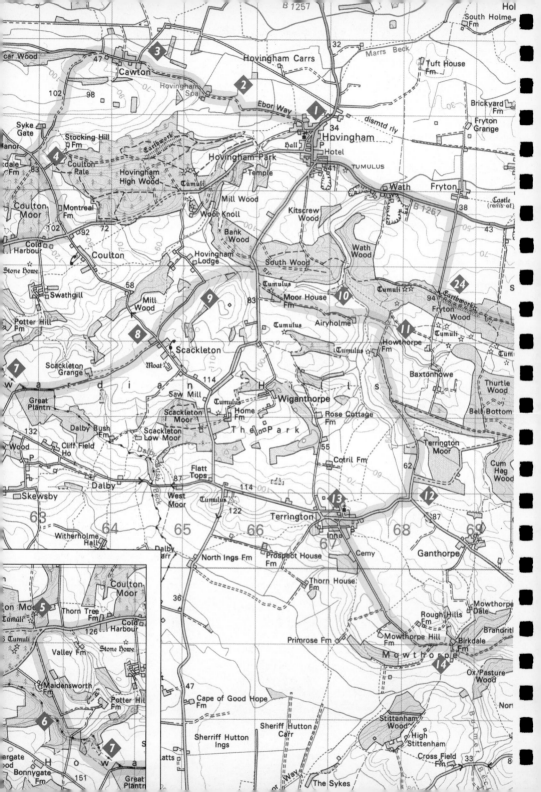

1 With back to the church in Hovingham L, then 1st road L. Follow the tarmac lane round to the R 'Rights of Way'. At the end of tarmac bear L onto broad stone track 'Bridleway, Ebor Way'

2 Follow main track (waymarked with blue arrows) as it swings R, then L past Spa House

3 At T-j with road bear L (in effect SA). Through Cawton and immediately after last cottages on the left (Rose Cottage and Hillcrest) bear L uphill onto broad track

4 At T-j with road, with stone house ahead, turn L. At X-roads by Give Way sign R 'Easingwold 7, Thirsk 16'

5 Ignore road to right to Helmsley. Take next road L 'Brandsby 2¼', then shortly 1st track L 'Bridleway'

6 Sandy track. **Easy to miss**. Track descends and swings L. Just before gateway bear R downhill 'Bridleway' (blue arrow). At tarmac R over bridge then immediately L alongside stream. At times overgrown. Muddy in winter

7 At T-j with broad stone track L into woodland

8 Track turns to tarmac near Scackleton Grange. At T-j by Scackleton L, then R

9 Long tarmac descent. **Easy to**

miss. As tarmac swings sharp L bear R (in effect SA) onto broad track along edge of field 'Bridleway' (blue arrow). Overgrown section. At T-j with road R, then 1st track L 'Airyholme. Bridleway'

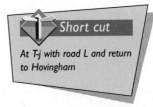

Short cut

At T-j with road L and return to Hovingham

10 Go past Moor House Farm on the right. Through gateway for Airyholme and just before barns/haystacks bear L away from stone track onto grassy track alongside fence

11 Through gates, along field edge. At T-j with broad track R. At T-j with farmhouse ahead L (blue arrow)

12 Fine gravel track. At T-j with road bear R (in effect SA) then shortly, at T-j, R 'Terrington ¾, Easingwold 11'

13 In Terrington 1st L onto Mowthorpe Lane 'No through road'

14 Tarmac turns to track and swings R past farm and through gates and shortly L downhill past pond

page 139

24 After 2 km (1½ miles) at X-roads with track/narrow tarmac lane turn R downhill. At T-j with B1257 L 'Hovingham' to return to the start. This last section will be busy

Places of interest

Hovingham 1
A fine example of an estate village planned with thought and taste. Its golden stone cottages stand among flowers, creepers and trim little greens at the massive entrance to Hovingham Hall, the home of the Duchess of Kent's family. Sir Thomas Worsley designed the hall in the mid-1700s and much of the credit for the elegance of the village must go to him

Sherriff Hutton 5 km (3 miles) south of 13
The village is dominated by the 14th-century castle ruin – once the seat of Richard III. Sherriff Hutton Hall was originally James I's hunting lodge. The grounds are open to the public

Castle Howard 3 km (2 miles) north of 16
Sir John Vanbrugh's design for the 3rd Earl of Carlisle features a vast dome above the entrance. Paintings include works by Van Dyck, Gainsborough and Reynolds. The grounds contain a 28 ha (70 acre) lake

Cycle Cycle Cycle
TOURS TOURS TOURS

The Ordnance Survey Cycle Tours series

os Ordnance Survey

Cycle

24 one-day routes in
The Yorkshire Dales

TOURS

Nick Cotton

- ◆ Around Birmingham
- ◆ Around London
- ◆ Avon, Somerset & Wiltshire
- ◆ Berks, Bucks & Oxfordshire
- ◆ Central Scotland
- ◆ Cornwall & Devon
- ◆ Cumbria & the Lakes
- ◆ Dorset, Hampshire & Isle of Wight
- ◆ East Anglia – South
- ◆ Gloucestershire and Hereford & Worcester
- ◆ Kent, Surrey & Sussex
- ◆ North Wales and The Marches
- ◆ North Yorkshire & Teesside
- ◆ Northumberland and County Durham
- ◆ Peak District
- ◆ Southern Scotland
- ◆ South, West and Mid-Wales
- ◆ Yorkshire Dales

*T*he whole series is available from all good bookshops or by mail order direct from the publisher. Payment can be made by credit card or cheque/postal order in the following ways:

By phone Phone your order through on our special *Credit Card Hotline* on *01733 371999 (Fax: 01733 370585)*. Speak to our customer service team during office hours (9am to 5pm) or leave a message on the answer machine, quoting your full credit card number plus expiry date and your full name and address and reference.

By post Simply fill out the order form (you may photcopy it) and send it to: *Reed Books Direct, 43 Stapledon Road, Orton Southgate, Peterborough PE2 6TD.*

Ordnance Survey Cycle **TOURS ORDER FORM**

I wish to order the following titles	Quantity @ £9.99 each		£ Total
AROUND BIRMINGHAM	[ ] 0 600 58623 5	➤	[ ]
AROUND LONDON	[ ] 0 600 58845 9	➤	[ ]
AVON, SOMERSET & WILTSHIRE	[ ] 0 600 58664 2	➤	[ ]
BERKS, BUCKS & OXFORDSHIRE	[ ] 0 600 58156 X	➤	[ ]
CENTRAL SCOTLAND	[ ] 0 600 59005 4	➤	[ ]
CORNWALL & DEVON	[ ] 0 600 58124 1	➤	[ ]
CUMBRIA & THE LAKES	[ ] 0 600 58126 8	➤	[ ]
DORSET, HAMPSHIRE & ISLE OF WIGHT	[ ] 0 600 58667 7	➤	[ ]
EAST ANGLIA – SOUTH	[ ] 0 600 58125 X	➤	[ ]
GLOUCESTERSHIRE AND HEREFORD & WORCESTER	[ ] 0 600 58665 0	➤	[ ]
KENT, SURREY & SUSSEX	[ ] 0 600 58666 9	➤	[ ]
NORTH WALES AND THE MARCHES	[ ] 0 600 59007 0	➤	[ ]
NORTH YORKSHIRE & TEESSIDE	[ ] 0 600 59103 4	➤	[ ]
NORTHUMBERLAND AND COUNTY DURHAM	[ ] 0 600 59105 0	➤	[ ]
PEAK DISTRICT	[ ] 0 600 58889 0	➤	[ ]
SOUTHERN SCOTLAND	[ ] 0 600 58624 3	➤	[ ]
SOUTH, WEST AND MID-WALES	[ ] 0 600 58846 7	➤	[ ]
YORKSHIRE DALES	[ ] 0 600 58847 5	➤	[ ]

Name...

Address...

....

....Postcode

I enclose a cheque/postal order, for a **total** of [ ]

made payable to *Reed Book Services*, or please debit my

☐ Access ☐ American Express ☐ Visa ☐ Diners

account by [ ]

Account no

☐☐☐☐ ☐☐☐☐ ☐☐☐☐ ☐☐☐☐

Expiry date ☐☐ ☐☐

◆ **Free postage and packing**

◆ All available titles will normally be dispatched within 5 working days of receipt of order but please allow up to 28 days for delivery

◆ Whilst every effort is made to keep prices low, the publisher reserves the right to increase prices at short notice

☐ Please tick this box if you do not wish your name to be used by other carefully selected organisations that may wish to send you information about other products and services

Registered Office: Michelin House, 81 Fulham Road, London SW3 6RB. Registered in England number 1974080

Signature...

Post to: Reed Books Direct, 43 Stapledon Road, Orton Southgate, Peterborough PE2 6TD